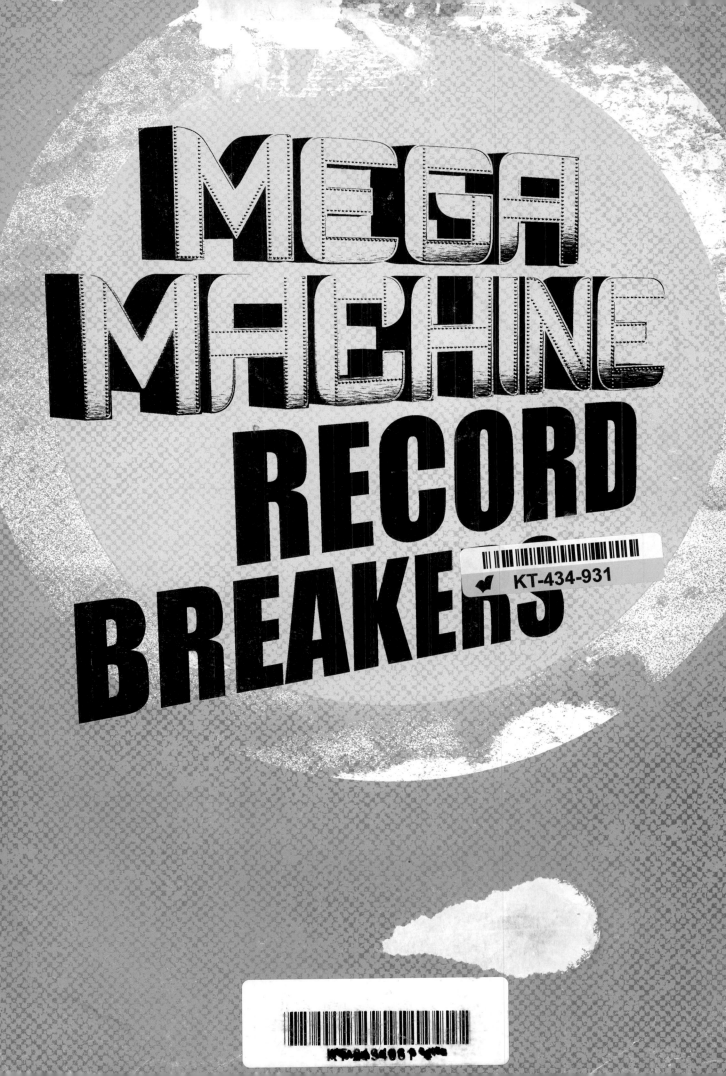

MEGA MACHINE RECORD BREAKERS

THIS IS A CARLTON BOOK

© Carlton Books Limited 2013

Author: Anne Rooney
Senior Editor: Anna Bowles
Senior Art Editor: Jake da'Costa
Design: Tall Tree
Cover Design: Jake da'Costa
Production: Ena Matagic

Anne Rooney asserts her moral rights to
be identified as the author of this work in
accordance with sections 77 and 78 of the
Copyright, Designs and Patents Act 1988.

Published in 2013 by Carlton Books Limited
An imprint of the Carlton Publishing Group
20 Mortimer Street, London, W1T 3JW

2 4 6 8 10 9 7 5 3

A catalogue record for this book is
available from the British Library.

ISBN 978 1 78312 005 5
Printed in Dubai

MEGA MACHINE
RECORD BREAKERS

>>>>>>>>>>>BIGGEST! <<<<<<<<<<<<<
>>>>>>>>>>>FASTEST! <<<<<<<<<<<<<
<<<<<<<<MOST POWERFUL! <<<

ANNE ROONEY

CARLTON
KiDS

CONTENTS

RECORD-BREAKING VEHICLES

RECORD BREAKERS

For thousands of years, no one could travel faster than a horse could gallop. The fastest vehicles were carts, carriages and sledges pulled by animals. It took months to cross a continent.

That was before we had engines. Then, around 250 years ago, a revolution began. A revolution that has given us trains, cars, planes, motorbikes, helicopters, submarines, dumper trucks, rollercoasters and much more.

ON THE MOVE

The very first powered vehicles were trains. They worked by burning coal to heat water, turning it to steam. The steam was used at high pressure to drive an engine, and that turned the wheels of the train. Later, trains were powered by diesel and then electricity. Now, super-fast electric trains travel at over 300 km/h, and **maglev** trains go even faster - over 400 km/h.

The Zefiro 380 maglev can reach an amaxing maximum speed of 380 km/h.

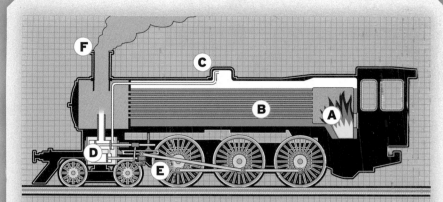

HOW A STEAM TRAIN WORKED

Hot gases from burning fuel in the firebox (**A**) go through tubes in the boiler (**B**). Water in the boiler turns to steam which collects in the steam dome (**C**). Steam is sent to the cylinders (**D**) where it drives a **piston**. The piston drives a connecting rod (**E**) which transmits power to the wheels. Waste steam and gases leave through the stack (**F**). Some of the steam will condense, and the gases go out here (directly from the pipes that have carried them through the boiler).

Formula 1 cars like this one are streamlined for maximum speed.

Space rockets need to burn heavy fuel to lift themselves off the ground.

ENGINES FOR EVERYONE

A train carries lots of people – but you can only go where the train is going. The invention of the internal combustion engine made personal transport possible. Cars and motorbikes used this type of engine. Power comes from burning a liquid fuel, such as petrol or diesel. The fastest cars can travel at 400 km/h.

LIFT OFF

The fastest cars have to be specially designed so that they don't lift off the ground. Engines can also take us off the ground deliberately. Fast, powerful planes use jet engines. As the engine burns fuel, waste gases pour from the back of the engine, creating a force which pushes the vehicle forwards. Space rockets work in the same way.

BIGGEST AND SMALLEST ENGINES

MONSTER MACHINE

Engine-powered vehicles range from massive supertankers to tiny collapsible motorbikes, from superfast rockets to giant earthmoving machines that crawl across the land.

The biggest diesel engines in the world power supertankers – huge ships that carry oil or freight. The Wärtsilä-Sulzer RTA96-C is a turbocharged two-stroke diesel engine, used in container ships. The biggest, 14-cylinder version is 13.5 m high, 27.3 m long, weighs over 2,300 tonnes (2,300,000 kg), and produces 80,080 kW of power.

⚙ SUPER POWERS

Concern about the impact on the environment of burning fossil fuels has led engineers to explore other power sources, too. Some vehicles are driven by electricity and some by solar power (from sunlight), wind power, hydrogen cells or biofuels – fuels made from waste plant and food matter.

The Pratt & Whitney F100 is a monster aircraft engine.

A ladder is needed to scale the engine, which is the size of a three-storey building.

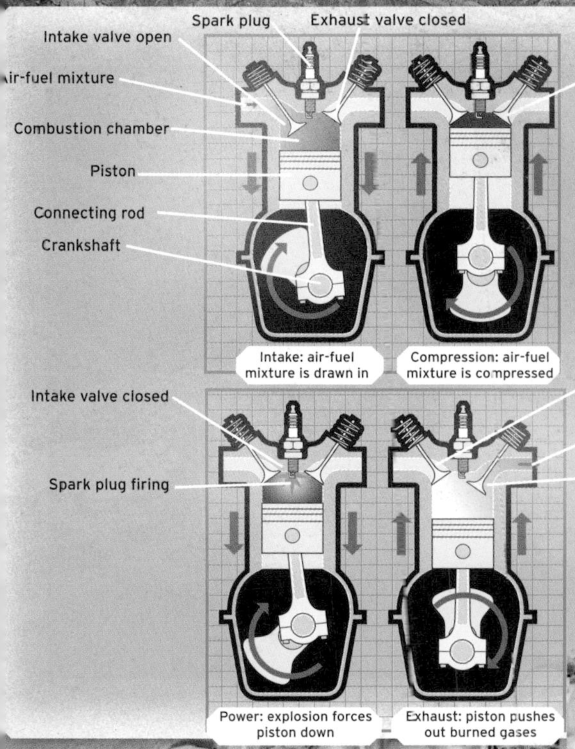

Diagram labels (engine cycle)

Spark plug
Exhaust valve closed
Intake valve open
Air-fuel mixture
Combustion chamber
Piston
Connecting rod
Crankshaft

Valves closed

Intake: air-fuel mixture is drawn in
Compression: air-fuel mixture is compressed

Intake valve closed
Spark plug firing

Intake valves closed
Exhaust gases
Exhaust valve open

Power: explosion forces piston down
Exhaust: piston pushes out burned gases

⚙ HOW CAR ENGINES WORK

Most cars and motorbikes use internal combustion engines. These create tiny explosions in an enclosed space. A fuel, such as petrol, is mixed with air and compressed in a chamber. A spark sets fire to the fuel. It burns explosively, pushing the **piston** at one end of the combustion chamber down. The movement of the piston is used to turn a crank. The piston goes up and down rapidly as the engine fires again and again, drawing in more fuel and air and setting light to it each time.

14 cylinders contain powerful pistons whose pumping motion is eventually translated into the movement of the ship.

Walkways surround the enormous engine to provide safe access for engineers.

⚙ MICRO MACHINE

The smallest vehicle engines are found in tiny, unmanned vehicles used for **surveillance**. Some of these crawl over the ground and others are mini-planes or helicopter-style drones. The tiniest are battery-powered. The Indian Tato Nano car has the smallest production petrol engine at 624 cc. It can drive the Nano at up to 105 kM/h.

nano

SMARTEST BIKE

FACTOR 001

A bicycle is a finely-tuned machine that works best if it is very light and aerodynamic and has parts that run smoothly and efficiently. But some bikes are smarter than others.

The Factor 001 has GPS and integrated **hydraulic**, electronic and lighting systems. It can work out the rider's body temperature and heartbeat and even how hard each leg is working. Each Factor 001 is custom-made and takes six engineers a week to make.

⚙ FASTEST BIKES

One of the fastest bikes has to be the Lotus 108 ridden by Chris Boardman in the 1992 Olympics in Barcelona. He covered 4 km in just over four minutes – an average speed of nearly 60 km/h. The bike has a solid back wheel, a three-spoke front wheel and very low handlebars to give the bike and rider an aerodynamic shape.

Fast bike, fast rider: Chris Boardman in 1992.

FACTOR 001

WHEN	2009
HOW FAST	113 KM/H
MADE BY	BERU f1 SYSTEMS
HOW HEAVY	7 KG
COST	£22,000

A carbon-fibre **monocoque** frame – a thin, curved, hollow shell – makes the bike super-strong and very light.

FACTOR001

bf1systems

FACTOR001

bf1

PARALYMPIC CYCLING

Special designs for cyclists with disabilities can be powered using the arms instead of the legs. Sometimes the bikes have three wheels for stability. One way of powering bikes like this is for the cyclist to pull on cables. It takes as much strength as riding a regular bike.

Hydraulic braking system with ceramic brakes.

Needle-thin wheels with untreaded tyres for grip and minimal **friction**.

YOU-POWERED

We don't think of bicycles as machines, but they are. Instead of being powered by petrol or diesel, they're powered by people! The fuel for your bicycle is the food you have eaten, converted to energy in your muscles. An Olympic track cyclist can generate almost 3 kW.

NIFTIEST MOTORBIKE

UNO

We usually think of motorbikes as big, powerful monsters – but some are small and nifty. The Uno looks like only half of a motorbike! It's powered by an electric motor, run by a battery recharged from the mains, making it quiet, non-polluting, and cheap to run.

The Uno III version has an additional small wheel that can come down, and the two large wheels can be moved closer together, converting it into a normal motorcycle. The bike can even switch between modes while in use. The inventor calls it 'the first real Transformer'.

⚙ FOLDING MOTORBIKE

The Yike Bike transforms even more than the Uno - it's a motorbike with a big front wheel and a tiny back wheel. But that strange shape folds away into a compact package that can be carried in the boot of a car or on a train. The Yike is powered by an electric engine, and with a single battery pack, it can travel 10 km between charges. Its top speed is 23kph.

A strong, light carbon-fibre and aluminium frame makes the Yike portable.

⚙ MINI MOTOS

Mini motos are tiny. Most have a two-stroke engine with a capacity of 39-50 cc. They're only about 50 cm high and a metre long. The smallest can reach speeds of 40 km/h, but they're not legal for road use.

A short body makes the bike easy to manoeuvre and gives it a tight turning circle.

Uses **gyro-technology** for speed control: leaning forward accelerates and leaning back slows it down

Two narrow wheels look from the side like a single wheel!

UNO

WHEN	2008
HOW FAST	40 KM/H
HOW HEAVY	58 KG
FUEL CONSUMPTION	ABOUT 50 KM ON 3-4 HOURS' CHARGE
ENGINE	ELECTRIC

FASTEST THING ON TWO WHEELS

TOP 1 ACK ATTACK

Not all vehicles are designed to go on the road. The fastest thing on two wheels is the TOP 1 Ack Attack, a specially designed motorbike made just to challenge the motorcycle world speed record.

The Ack Attack doesn't look like a motorbike because it's completely covered in an aerodynamic shell to make it cut through the air easily. It broke the world record on the Bonneville Salt Flats, Utah, USA in 2010 travelling at 605.697 km/h.

Rider is enclosed inside the vehicle shell, keeping the shape uninterrupted.

Streamlined shape like a bullet that is low to the ground to increase traction and reduce **drag**.

WWW.TOPOIL.COM

$ SUZUKI

DRAG-BIKE RACING

Drag bikes are customized for speed. Often, the **suspension** is lowered to increase traction and special exhaust pipes give the bike more 'kick'. The race is over in seconds, covering only 400 m, and riders have to balance speed against road-holding with lightning-quick responses to the bike's performance. Bikes set off in pairs, racing against each other, with the winner going on to compete again. Pro drag-riders wear leathers made of kangaroo hide - it's tougher than cow leather and gives more protection in a fall.

FASTEST ON THE ROAD

You won't see the Ack Attack on the roads, but you might just see the fastest production motorbike, the Suzuki Hayabusa. It can travel at up to 303 km/h, using a 1,299-cc engine that delivers 128.4 kW. The Hayabusa will remain unchallenged in Europe as new regulations have set a top speed capability of 300 km/h, with bikes limited electronically so that they can't go faster.

The Hayabusa can accelerate to 306 km/h in under 10 seconds.

WHAT MAKES A MOTORBIKE FAST?

An engine that delivers a lot of power is obviously important for speed. But that's not all that matters. The vehicle must also have a streamlined shape - one that moves through the air (or water, for boats) easily without bits that stick out and create drag. For a motorbike or bicycle, the rider's position matters, too. A rider sitting upright impairs the streamlining. That's why riders crouch low over the handlebars.

Carbon-fibre body built on a chrome-molybdenum frame.

TOP 1 ACK ATTACK

WHEN	2010
HOW HEAVY	727 KG
TOP SPEED	606.697 KM/H
POWER	671 KW
ENGINE	2600 CC - TWO SUZUKI HAYABUSA TURBOCHARGED ENGINES

MOST RUGGED QUAD BIKE

YAMAHA RAPTOR 700R

Yamaha Raptor 700R quad bikes have won four Dakar Rallies – the longest annual rally in the world over almost 10,000 km of harsh terrain.

Quad bikes, or all-terrain vehicles (ATVs), are a cross between a motorbike and a car. They have four wheels like a car, but a single rider, handlebars and no roof or crash bar. They're designed for rough terrain, and extreme quad-bike rallies run over deserts, mud, hills or ice and snow.

⚙ BIG BEAST OF A BIKE

The biggest quad bike in the world is the Can Am Outlander 1000. With a 976-cc engine that can produce 60.3 kW and suspension that allows a lot of movement, it can power through the most terrible conditions. The **airbox** is high on the **chassis** to avoid sucking in too much water, mud and sand, and it filters the air before sending it to the engine. Engine braking helps slow the bike going downhill so it doesn't hurtle out of control.

Up to 25 cm wheel-travel deals with bumps and hollows.

Steel and aluminium chassis for a super-strong structure.

⚙ UP AND OVER

If hammering through mud isn't good enough, quad bikes can also be used for jumping. The longest ramp jump on a quad bike was 53.92 m, a record set in Australia in 2008 by American Jon Guetter.

686-cc four-stroke engine is optimised for torque – turning force – to make the Raptor stable and easy to manoeuvre.

YAMAHA RAPTOR 700R

WHEN	2006-12
HOW HEAVY	191 KG
ENGINE	686-CC FOUR-STROKE

⚙ TORQUE

Torque is a measure of rotational force. The torque determines the force with which the wheels of a vehicle can be turned, while the energy the engine can generate (in kW) is a measure of its power. A challenge for vehicles that run over difficult terrain is to turn the wheels with enough force to go up steep slopes and over uneven ground. A quad bike needs high torque at low rpm (revolutions per minute – how fast the engine turns) as it's not aiming to go fast but to stick to the ground.

BIGGEST BIKE

MONSTER MOTORBIKE

The Monster Motorbike weighs 13.6 tonnes and is 3 m tall. Ray Baumann, who built the bike in Perth, Australia, uses it to perform stunts, crushing cars and caravans under its wheels.

The diesel truck engine has been adapted to be more like a regular bike engine. There's also an automatic gearbox from a lorry and a **differential** from an **articulated** lorry that drives a massive chain on each side of the rear wheel.

Kevlar-like body plates for protection.

The wheels taken from a Caterpillar 80-tonne excavator have tyres 3 m tall that each weigh 2,700 kg.

⚙ BIGGEST YOU CAN BUY

The largest production motorbike is the Boss Hoss BHC-3 502 Big Block. Boss bikes have Chevrolet V8 engines with a capacity of up to 8,226 cc (8.2 litres). But what is 'biggest'? The bike with the most powerful engine or the bike that takes up most space? The Gunbus 410 has a smaller engine at 6,728 cc but weighs 650 kg, while the Big Boss weighs just under 500 kg.

MONSTER MOTORBIKE

WHEN	2008
HOW HEAVY	13.6 TONNES
SIZE	9.14 M LONG; 3 M TALL
ENGINE	DETROIT DIESEL TRUCK ENGINE

HEAVY METAL

The heaviest motorbike in the world is the 4,749 kg Harzer Bike Schmiede. It was built by Tilo and Wilfried Niebel in Germany and took a team of mechanics and welders a year to make. It's 5.28 m long and 2.29 m tall and is powered by an engine taken from an old Russian tank.

The seat and frame are from a Honda motorbike. A **pneumatic** arm raises the seat to its driving position when the engine is on.

The bike's huge engine is shown here, with the Russian emblem.

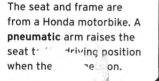

MONSTER MOTORBIKE from HELL

SIZE AND POISE

To stop the Monster Motorbike tipping over, there's a sump guard that weighs 1,180 kg, plus a metal plate beneath it that's 2.5 cm thick and weighs 1,200 kg. It's just 12.5 cm off the ground, so it keeps the bike's centre of gravity low.

The Monster Motorbike weighs the same as 10 family cars!

SPEEDIEST SPORTS CAR

BUGATTI VEYRON

With a top speed of 432 km/h, the Bugatti Veyron Super Sport is the fastest street-legal car in the world. It's a beautiful luxury sports car that can go so fast it needs special features to prevent it lifting off the road!

Jeremy Clarkson of the BBC programme Top Gear called the Veyron "The greatest car ever made and the greatest car we will ever see in our lifetime." The car can be legally driven at top speed only in countries with no maximum speed limit.

At speeds above 200 km/h, the back wing is also used as an **air brake** like those that help to slow aeroplanes.

⚙ GET READY FOR SPEED

The Veyron's everyday top speed (in 'handling mode') is 350 km/h. When it reaches 220 km/h, the car adapts automatically. Hydraulics lower the body to reduce the ground clearance to 9 cm and the wing and spoiler deploy. The wing provides 3,425 N of force to hold the car down on the road. If the driver turns on 'top speed mode', it can go even faster. The car checks that the driver and car are ready and safe, then the spoiler retracts, the front air diffusers shut and ground clearance drops to 6.5 cm.

⚙ GOING...

The Veyron has an 8-litre, quad-turbocharged, W16 cylinder engine. This is the equivalent of two V8 engines placed side-by-side. A V8 has eight cylinders arranged in pairs so that they make four v-shapes. The pistons of the cylinders all drive the same **crankshaft**. As the pistons move in sequence, they push against the crankshaft and make it turn.

BUGATTI VEYRON SUPER SPORT

WHEN	2005
HOW HEAVY	1,888 KG
TOP SPEED	432 KM/H
ACCELERATION	0-100 KM/H IN 2.5 SECONDS
COST	£2,000,000
POWER	736 KW
ENGINE	7,993 CC

At very high speeds, hydraulics lower the chassis to keep the car on the road – otherwise lift might make it take off.

BUGATTI

The W16 engine has four **turbochargers**. A turbocharger sucks air into the engine so that it can use fuel more quickly and generate more power.

MOST POPULAR CAR

VOLKSWAGEN BEETLE

The best-selling car of all time is the Volkswagen Beetle: more than 21 million have been built in the past 65 years.

The Beetle was invented as a car for the people – 'volkswagen' means 'people's car'. In 1933, the German government asked Porsche to develop an affordable car that could carry two adults and three children at 100 km/h. The Second World War started while they were still making prototypes and the first production Beetles were not made until 1946.

The engine is at the back, in the boot, and the car has rear-wheel drive – an unusual combination when the car was first designed.

⚙ FIRST MASS-PRODUCED CAR

The first truly affordable car was the Model T Ford: 15 million were built in the USA from 1908 to 1927. It was the first car to be made on a production line, each worker carrying out only one task. Cars could be built very quickly – one was finished every 15 minutes. The Model T had a 2,900-cc engine that produced 15 kW and could reach a top speed of 64-72 km/h. The earliest models were started with a crank handle.

VOLKSWAGEN BEETLE	
WHEN	1946
TOP SPEED	100 KM/H
POWER	19 KW
ENGINE	995 CC

⚙ DESIGNED AND REDESIGNED

The Beetle has been through several redesigns and has been built in lots of countries besides Germany. But it still has a distinctive humped shape and an engine in the rear boot. A new soft-top convertible launched in 2013 – but the first soft-top was issued in 1949.

Beetles were built in Mexico from 1939-2003.

The original Beetle was nearly airtight and could float on water for a few minutes.

KS-VW 57

⚙ "ANY COLOUR AS LONG AS IT'S BLACK."

The Model T Ford was available only in black until 1926 – because the only type of paint that would dry quickly enough to use on the production line was a black lacquer called 'Japan black'. When better paints were invented, other colours became available.

SMALLEST CAR

PEEL P50

The tiniest production car ever made was the Peel P50. This three-wheeled microcar was made by Peel Engineering Company on the Isle of Man in 1962-65.

With its four-stroke 49 cc petrol engine mounted in the side, the P50 could manage 60 km/h. It had no starter motor and the driver had to use a crank handle to get it going. The P50 could be parked in a small space, but with no reverse gear it was often easier to get out and move it by hand. Just 50 P50s were made – 27 still exist.

Single headlight, single windscreen-wiper and just one door – it had room for 'one adult and a shopping bag'.

⚙ POSTMAN PAT REVAMPED

The smallest ever drivable car is the Wind-Up, made by British engineer Perry Watkins in 2009. It's made from a converted Postman Pat coin-in-the-slot ride and is 132 cm long, 104 cm tall and 66 cm wide. The fibreglass body is reinforced with a steel frame and there's a mini quad-bike with a 150 cc engine underneath.

⚙ HYDROGEN FUEL CELL

A hydrogen fuel cell is rather like a battery except that it never runs out.
Hydrogen enters the cell, where it breaks down to make electrons and hydrogen ions. The electrons produce the electric power and the hydrogen ions combine with oxygen to make water, which is the only waste product.

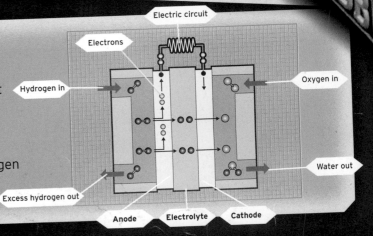

Electric circuit

Electrons

Hydrogen in

Oxygen in

Water out

Excess hydrogen out

Anode   Electrolyte   Cathode

Fibreglass body available in red, white or blue.

PEEL P50

HOW HEAVY	59 KG
TOP SPEED	60 KM/H
POWER	2.5 KW
ENGINE	49 CC

A handle on the rear made it easy to drag it around - or it could be pulled by the front bumper.

⚙ SMALL AND EFFICIENT

The most fuel efficient car is the experimental PAC-Car II. Running on a hydrogen fuel cell, it uses only 1 g of hydrogen per 100 km. That's equivalent to 5,385 km per litre! The PAC-Car II could go three times round the world on the petrol Concorde used on the runway before take-off.

FASTEST RACERS

TOP-FUEL DRAGSTER

The fastest racing cars on Earth are top-fuel dragsters. They have the fastest acceleration of any land vehicle, going from 0 to 200 km/h in less than a second.

Dragsters race over very short distances. The race starts with a burst of flame and a roar of engines and is over in five or six seconds! Dragsters race in pairs, with the winner going on to compete again. It's not just a race to the finish: electronics monitor reaction time (how long it takes the driver to start), the time taken to cover the track and top speed. The winner is the car to finish in the shortest time.

⚙ ON YOUR MARKS...

Before the race starts, the cars perform a 'burnout'. They drive over the start of the track, heating up the tyres and laying down a thin film of rubber on the road. It makes the tyres and road sticky, increasing traction for the wheels.

Each car lays down its own non-slip slick of rubber at burnout.

⚙ PIMP MY RIDE

Although top-fuel dragsters are designed for speed, amateur drag racing has lots of cars designed to look wacky as well as go fast.

TOP-FUEL DRAGSTERS	
TOP SPEED	483 KM/H
ACCELERATION	0-200 KM/H IN LESS THAN A SECOND
POWER (KW)	5,966 KW
ENGINE	8.9 LITRE

A rear wing catches the air and prevents the car lifting off the road.

After the race, parachutes are used to slow the car down and avoid excessive wear on the carbon-fibre brakes.

⚙ LOOKING INSIDE

The engine is typically a supercharged V8. The supercharger forces air at higher than atmospheric pressure against the pistons, increasing the power the engine generates. A dragster can get through 5 litres of rocket fuel (nitromethane) a second and generates a force of 5G – five times the force of gravity! Fuel is pumped into the pistons so fast there isn't time for it all to burn, so some is expelled while still burning.

Burning fuel mixed with waste gases produce dramatic jets of fire.

FASTEST TRUCK

SHOCKWAVE

The world's fastest truck, called Shockwave, is powered by three jet aircraft engines. It can reach a top speed of 605 km/h. Shockwave is used in dramatic displays, racing jet aircraft that fly above it – and winning!

Shockwave has three Pratt & Whitney J34-48 engines normally used in planes. They produce as much thrust as the Space Shuttle, so even though Shockwave is heavy it's in danger of lifting. The engines are arranged in a pyramid, slightly tilted to help keep the truck on the ground.

Tyres each have 38.5 kg of tread shaved away to reduce the mass of the truck and prevent the tread ripping away at high speeds.

⚙ LEAN, MEAN AND GREEN

Running a truck like Shockwave takes a lot of fuel – but the Volvo Mean Green lets truck-lovers enjoy a less fuel-hungry ride. Mean Green is built from standard Volvo truck components, including a highly tuned D16 engine, but it also has an electric motor. A hybrid vehicle combines power from standard fuels such as diesel or petrol with power from another source – usually electricity, solar or wind power. The Mean Green uses diesel for most of its power, but nearly 10% comes from an electric motor. It can reach 236 km/h.

Mean Green is the fastest hybrid truck on the planet.

Piezoelectric ignitors set fire to unburned diesel escaping the exhaust stacks and the engine outlet to make dramatic flames.

⚙ TRUCK RACING

The FIA (Fédération Internationale de l'Automobile) runs Grand Prix truck-racing events for two-axle articulated truck tractors. With 12-litre tubocharged diesel engines that deliver 894 kW, two-axle trucks weighing over 5,500 kg compete at speeds up to 160 km/h. The minimum weight limit stops mechanics replacing standard parts with lighter metals. The speed is capped for safety reasons, so the trucks compete on handling – especially overtaking on corners – and acceleration and braking. They're not quite the same trucks as you see on the roads, as they've been highly tuned to give excellent acceleration.

The engine runs on diesel – but it's not very fuel efficient. It burns about 500 litres per kilometre!

WORLD LAND SPEED RECORD

THRUST SSC

The fastest land vehicle on Earth is the Thrust SSC (Supersonic Car), specially built just to smash the landspeed record, which it did in 1997 by going at 1,228 km/h.

Thrust's twin **turbojet** engines are the same as those used in Phantom fighter planes and the Thrust SSC looks more like a wingless plane than a car. The engines produce a combined thrust of 223,000 N. It was the first land vehicle to break the sound barrier.

Engine at the front so that its weight helps to keep the car on the ground.

Two wheels slightly out of alignment – one is a little in front of the other to make room for rear-wheel drive mechanism in the narrow rear.

Two giant Rolls Royce turbojet engines produce more power than 1,000 family saloon cars put together.

MIDNIGHT SUN VII

WHEN	2004
HOW HEAVY	213 KG
TOP SPEED	130 KM/H
SIZE	1.5 M x 5.5 M

⚙ SUN IN SPACE

In space, sunlight is available all the time and is much stronger than on Earth. Satellites often use solar panels to provide the power they need to run electrical equipment. They can be angled to catch the most sunlight as the satellite moves through space.

⚙ CATCHING THE SUN

Midnight Sun X has 403 Sun Power A300 solar cells with a total sun-trapping area of 6m². The energy caught by the solar cells is stored in a lithium polymer battery.

Aluminium frame and a Kevlar-composite body make the car light but strong.

Craft with solar sails could waft between planets.

⚙ SAILING IN THE SUN

NASA is looking at ways of propelling spacecraft very long distances through space. As there is no air resistance in space, a tiny amount of thrust can move a vehicle a long way. One possibility is solar sails. As photons fall on the sail, they push the vehicle through space, just like wind pushes a yacht over the water.

QUICKEST WIND-POWERED VEHICLE

ECOTRICITY GREENBIRD

It's not really a car and it's not really a boat – the Ecotricity Greenbird is a land yacht. It's powered by wind, which is caught in its sails, and it's driven over the land just like a yatch is driven over water. It broke the world record for land yachts by travelling at 203 km/h in Nevada, USA, in 2009.

The key to its success is its combination of aircraft and Formula 1 design elements. Just as the force of wind under an aircraft wing keeps the plane in the air, so the force of wind behind the Greenbird's sail drives it forward. It has wheels in the nose, beneath the tail and under the **outrigger**.

The position of the sail is controlled by a tail, attached to it with a rod. The wind pushes on the tail and the movement is conveyed from the rod to the sail.

⚙ TURN AROUND

Another way of harnessing wind power uses the wind to drive a turbine rather than push on a sail. It uses the same principle as a windmill or wind turbine, but instead of powering a mill or a generator, it drives a vehicle.

An outrigger on a long arm prevents the Greenbird being overturned by the force of wind against the sail.

RACING BOATS ON LAND

Races for land yachts use the wind to power a vehicle that looks more like a boat than Greenbird. These land yachts have flexible [sail]s and no outrigger. The faster the boat, the wider the wheel [bas]e needed to stop the yacht tipping over.

Yacht races aren't limited to the water!

ecotricity

GONE WITH THE WIND

The Greenbird's streamlined shape and efficient design mean it can run faster than the wind that is blowing it - up to five times as fast as the wind speed, in fact. The sail must be angled to keep the wind on the right side, pushing the vehicle forwards. An adapted version of the Greenbird can run on ice. The ice version has a different nose and skates instead of wheels.

ECOTRICITY GREENBIRD

WHEN	2009
HOW HEAVY	600 KG
TOP SPEED	203 KM/H
ENGINE	none

It's made entirely from carbon-fibre composite - the only metal is in the wheel units and wing bearings.

greenbird

LONGEST CABLE CAR

TATEV AERIAL TRAMWAY

The longest cable car ride in the world is Tatev aerial tramway in Armenia. It spans the Vorotan River Gorge, linking the village of Halizor and the medieval Tatev Monastery – a distance of 5,752 m. It can travel at 37 km/h.

The system has two cars that travel along cables suspended over the ground to carry passengers up the mountain. There are three support towers between the terminals. At its highest the tramway is 300 m above the ground. The two cars can each carry 25 passengers. As one car goes up, the other comes down.

The cars have no engines, but hang from a propulsion cable by a grip and are pulled along with the cable.

⚙ SCARIEST

Perhaps the scariest cable car ride in the world is at Heaven's Gate Mountain (Tianmen Chan) in China. Strictly speaking, it's not a cable car but a gondola. It soars above a breathtaking mountain gorge travelling up a height of 1,279 m over a run of 7,455 m and at times reaching an angle of 38 degrees. Swaying above the forest in a tiny metal capsule – that's got to be scary.

The cables run in straight lines as the cars can't turn corners – they can't decouple from the propualsion wire to go round a wheel in the way gondola ski lifts turn corners.

⚙ EVEN LONGER

Norsjö aerial tramway (right) is a 13.2 km aerial tramway in Sweden, but no longer runs regularly. It was built in the 1940s to move metal ore around a mining district. The cabins can each hold four people. The cars travel at a top speed of 10 km/h and take one hour and 45 minutes to complete the journey.

Huge winches powered by electric engines wind a loop of propulsion cable, which pulls the cars along.

AMERIAGROUP

2

⚙ QUICK ESCAPE!

Rocket launch sites often have cable car escape systems that can take launch staff and astronauts away from a launch that is going wrong. The cable car takes them down from the launch tower to a protective shelter.

TATEV AERIAL TRAMWAY

WHEN	2010
TOP SPEED	37 KM/H
SIZE	5,752 M

FASTEST ROLLERCOASTER

FORMULA ROSSA

The fastest rollercoaster in the world is the Formula Rossa at Ferrari World theme park in Abu Dhabi – by a long way! It's 40km/h faster than previous rollercoasters, taking just 4.9 seconds to get from 0 to its top speed of 240 km/h.

The train is launched with as much force as the catapult on an aircraft carrier launches jets. The feeling of being in the train is as close to being in a Formula 1 car as possible. Riders have to wear goggles like those worn by skydivers to protect their eyes from sand, dust and insects.

⚙ HYDRAULIC POWER

Rollercoasters use hydraulic launchers to blast the trains down the track. Hydraulic fluid is pumped into **accumulators** that have two compartments separated by a piston. As hydraulic fluid is pumped into one compartment, gas in the other is compressed. At launch, the accumulators simultaneously release their stored power to drive 16 or 32 hydraulic motors. These spin a winch that rewinds a cable connected to a catch-car under the train. The catch-car moves along a groove in the launch track. A launch can have a peak power of 15,000 kW – as much as nearly 120 family cars!

The speed and acceleration on the ride are the same as in a Ferrari Formula 1 race car – passengers feel 4.8 times the force of gravity.

2.09 km of track is covered in a run that takes only 92 seconds.

FORMULA ROSSA	
WHEN	2010
TOP SPEED	240 KM/H
ACCELERATION	0-100 KM/H IN 2 SECONDS
SIZE	2.07 KM TRACK

The train is launched by hydraulic motors, then immediately climbs a 53 m hill, when it's then slowed down by magnetic brakes.

UPSIDE DOWN AND INSIDE OUT

The Formula Rossa focuses on speed, but the Colossus rollercoaster at Thorpe Park, England, concentrates on twists and turns. It has more inversions – when passengers are upside-down – than any other rollercoaster in the world, with a vertical loop, a cobra roll, two corkscrews and five heartline twists.

Record-breaking ups and downs on the Colossus.

GOING DOWN!

The rollercoaster with the biggest drop is Kingda Ka at Six Great Flags Adventure in Jackson, USA. The coaster cars are launched at such force they reach a speed of 206 km/h in three seconds.

At the end of the launch track they whizz up a 'top hat' tower 139 m tall and then plummet straight down for 127 m! The whole ride takes only 28 seconds.

LARGEST LIMO

MIDNIGHT RIDER

The largest limo in the world is the Midnight Rider, a tractor-trailer limousine pimped to perfection.

As well as three downstairs lounges decorated with brass and polished wood, there's a bronze staircase up to an observation lounge. Midnight Rider has a full bar, four landline phone connections, climate control heating and air conditioning – and a security monitoring system. With its own generators, all the electrical equipment works when the engine is not running.

The limousine comes with a staff of five – a bartender, a hostess, two drivers, and an engineer.

MIDNIGHT RIDER

HOW HEAVY	22,934 KG
SIZE	21.33 M LONG
POWER	324 KW

BIG, BUT SMALL

It sounds crazy but there are even limos made from Minis. Minis are small and limos are big, but by adding enough extra space to the middle of a Mini, it can be turned into a limo.

22 low-profile wheels with air ride suspension give a smooth ride.

The American Dream limo is an amazing 30.5 m long.

LONGEST LIMO

The longest limo in the world is the American Dream. Inside, it has a jacuzzi, a swimming pool with a diving board, a double bed and a satellite dish. Outside, there's a helipad and a sun deck. It has driver's compartments front and rear - the rear one is used for reversing. It's not street legal, so it's transported to events on two trucks and joined back together at the destination.

Seats 40 passengers in three lounges, each equipped with large satellite TV screens and entertainment systems, movies, music and live feeds.

SWANKY!

Limousines are usually made by extending a car and fitting it out with extra seats and lots of facilities. Some have comfy sofas, plasma screens, bars, dining tables and beds. They don't go very fast, as the extra work goes on making the inside extravagant rather than tuning the engine. Often, a camera sends images to the driver of the rear of the vehicle

SAFEST CAR

The car is marked up with stickers. Comparing the relative positions of the stickers before and after the crash shows how much the metal has distorted.

VOLVO V40

The safest car in the world is the Volvo V40. Cars are crash-tested by... being crashed. All kinds of high-speed collisions are simulated in crash-test centres, and the damage to the car and fake occupants – crash-test dummies – is carefully measured.

With two adult dummies in the front and two child-sized dummies in the back, the Volvo V40 was driven into a pile of crash blocks at 64 km/h. The front of the car was mashed up – but the 'driver' and 'passengers' were protected by crumple zones, **airbags** and seat belts. The computer analysis showed they had no significant risk of injury.

⚙ CAREFUL CAR

The Volvo V40 has some very special safety features. The pedestrian-detection system can spot a person stepping into the road and warn the driver. If the driver doesn't respond, the car brakes automatically. And if a pedestrian is struck, the bonnet opens and an airbag protects the pedestrian.

The V40 on the road.

VOLVO V40

WHEN	2012
TOP SPEED	250 KM/H
ACCELERATION	0-100 KM/H IN 6.7 SECONDS
SIZE	4.37 M LONG
POWER	132 KW
ENGINE	TURBO-CHARGED T4 1.6 litre PETROL ENGINE (T4 MODEL)

⚙ TESTING, TESTING

Test cars are crashed in different ways, simulating the car crashing into something in front of it, being struck from behind and the sides and rolling over. Cameras film the car from all angles, both inside and outside the vehicle. Slowing down the footage recorded enables engineers to see exactly what happens in a crash test.

The rigid body does not give way under impact, except for special crumple zones that absorb the shock.

Airbags inflate on impact to protect driver and passengers, including extra airbags at the sides of the car and near the driver's legs. An external airbag protects any pedestrian struck by the car.

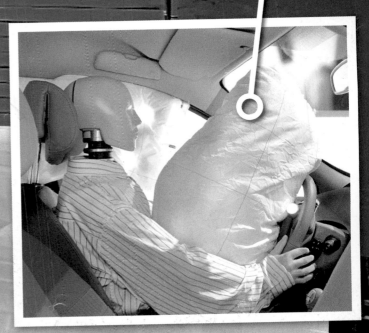

⚙ DUMMY!

The aim of making a car safe is to protect the people in it and, as far as possible, pedestrians on the road. Crash-test centres use dummies the same weight, size and shape as humans, and their body parts have the same weight distribution. They are fitted with monitors and sensors to collect data about forces operating on them during the impact.

STRANGEST CUSTOM CARS

DODGE POWER WAGON

The world's biggest car is a scaled-up Dodge Power Wagon built at a scale of 64:1. It belongs to Sheikh Hamad Al Nahyan of the United Arab Emirates.

The wheels of the Dodge are from an oil rig transporter and the wipers from an ocean liner. The headlights cost £1,000 each. It's equipped as a gigantic motorhome, with four bedrooms inside. It's so big that the pieces had to be taken out into the desert for assembly. The Dodge can be driven through empty desert but is too wide to use on a road.

The tailgate opens to form a balcony for the rooms inside the Dodge.

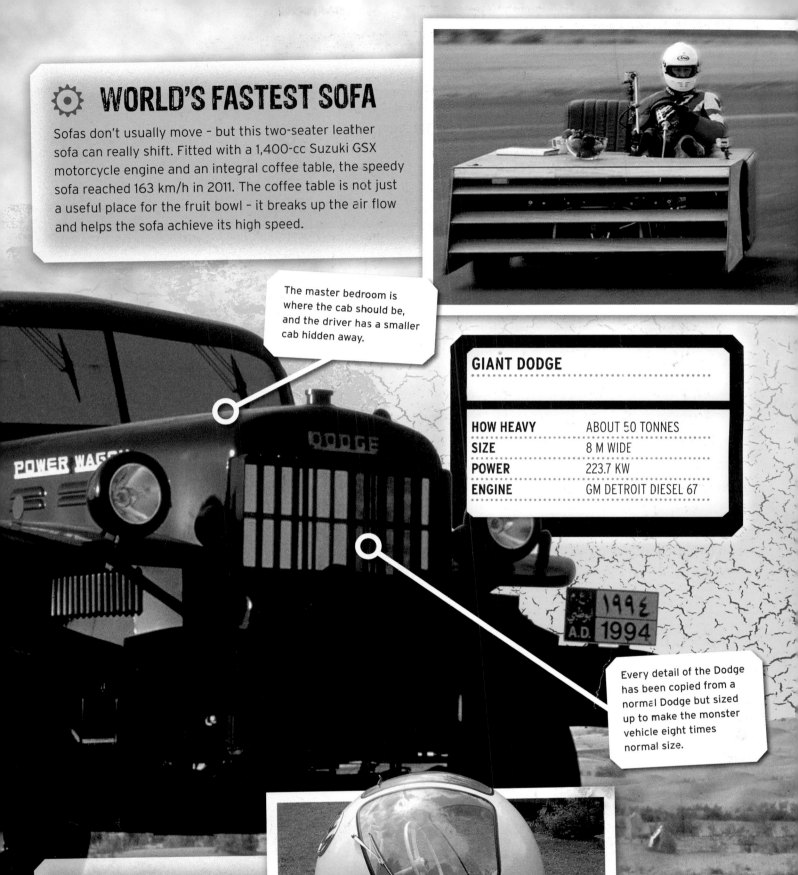

⚙ WORLD'S FASTEST SOFA

Sofas don't usually move - but this two-seater leather sofa can really shift. Fitted with a 1,400-cc Suzuki GSX motorcycle engine and an integral coffee table, the speedy sofa reached 163 km/h in 2011. The coffee table is not just a useful place for the fruit bowl - it breaks up the air flow and helps the sofa achieve its high speed.

The master bedroom is where the cab should be, and the driver has a smaller cab hidden away.

POWER WAGON

DODGE

GIANT DODGE	
HOW HEAVY	ABOUT 50 TONNES
SIZE	8 M WIDE
POWER	223.7 KW
ENGINE	GM DETROIT DIESEL 67

١٩٩٤
A.D. 1994

Every detail of the Dodge has been copied from a normal Dodge but sized up to make the monster vehicle eight times normal size.

⚙ CRAZY CARS

Custom cars are pimped-up cars that often look wacky on the outside and have surprisingly powerful engines hidden inside.

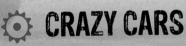

This VW Bus Ball has a door and driving seat but not wheels.

MOST LUXURIOUS MOTORHOME

ELEMMENT PALAZZO

The amazing Marchi Mobile eleMMent Palazzo is the most luxurious production motorhome ever made.

The sumptuous insides include a kitchen, lounge area with a metre-wide flat-screen satellite TV and en-suite bedroom. There's a a pop-up roof terrace, underfloor heating and a space-age driver's cockpit. There's even remote video access to show it off and remote control to turn on the heating and lighting before you get home.

At the press of a button, the side moves outwards to give 80% more floor space – and there's even a pop-up roof terrace called the 'sky lounge'.

⚙ MOTORHOME ON THE WATER

The Terra Wind is an amphibious motorhome – it can go on the land or in the water. It weighs 15,875 kg and is nearly 13 m long. Powered by a 246 kW Caterpillar diesel engine, it can go at 137 km/h on land, or 7 knots on water. It can handle waves up to nearly a metre high and winds up to 64 km/h. The inside is luxurious, with TVs, DVD and a surround-sound system, whirlpool bath tub and a swimming deck.

The Terra Wind is the world's first amphibious coach.

MARCHI MOBILE ELEMMENT PALAZZO

HOW HEAVY	20 TONNES
TOP SPEED	150 KM/H
FUEL CONSUMPTION	5.5 KM/LITRE
SIZE	12 M LONG
COST	$3,000,000
POWER	395 KW

It combines lots of luxury vehicles, with the rear diffuser of a sports car, the gangway of a business jet and the **flybridge** of a motor yacht.

The space-age aerodynamic design reduces fuel consumption by 20% and the glow-in-the-dark paint detailing makes it really stand out – even in the dark.

LONGEST BUS

AUTOTRAM EXTRA

The longest ever bus is the AutoTram Extra first run in Dresden, Germany, which is 30.7 m long. The 'bendy bus' is cheaper to use than a normal tram, which runs on rails built into the road.

The bus is a hybrid: it has electric and diesel power. The lithium ion battery (on the roof of the second car) can run the bus for 8 km; then the diesel engine kicks in, recharging the batteries as it runs the bus.

Walk-through bendy joints between the three compartments make it as easy to manoeuvre as an ordinary bus.

⚙ LOOK – NO HANDS!

At the opposite extreme, the very short Park Shuttle in Amsterdam has a single compartment - and no driver. It uses no mechanical guidance, such as rails or overhead lines. Instead, it has a stored map of the location and compares its position with this, counting revolutions of the wheels to track how far it has gone. Magnets in the road are used by an onboard computer to check the position every now and then.

The tiny Park Shuttle is only a bit longer than a family car.

ROAD AND RAIL

The DMV Bus Train, recently tested in Japan, combines the best of bus and train. It has two sets of wheels – steel wheels for using on the railway track and rubber-tyred wheels for using on the road. The driver can switch between wheels sets by lowering one and raising the other.

AUTOTRAM EXTRA	
WHEN	2012
HOW HEAVY	42,235 KG
SIZE	30.7 M
COST	£778,000
POWER	455 KW (DIESEL); 420 KW (CAPACITORS); 120 KW BATTERY (ELECTRIC)

96 seats and room for 160 standing passengers – the capacity of a small train.

The first multi-axle steering system ever used in a bus, gives the AutoTram a turning radius of 12.5 metres, which is less than some shorter buses.

CORNERING A BENDY BUS

At the connections between carriages, the AutoTram has a universal joint with hinges on the side furthest from the driver's cab. As the bus turns, one side of the joint is brought closer to the carriage in front and the other side pushed further away.

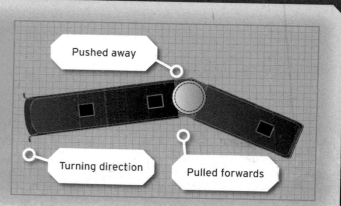

Pushed away

Turning direction

Pulled forwards

QUICKEST
ICE EXPLORER

BIO-INSPIRED ICE VEHICLE

You might have slid over snow on a sledge – but imagine whizzing at 130 km/h over the polar ice. The Bio-Inspired Ice Vehicle (BIV) skates over the snow on skids that look like fat skis. It's light enough to be dragged over the huge waves of snow found in some parts of Antarctica.

The BIV is not only the fastest ice-going vehicle – it was also used in 2012 in a record-breaking crossing of Antarctica, only the third-ever land crossing. It's also the first biofuel-powered vehicle ever to reach the South Pole.

Extremely low temperatures are punishing for mechanical equipment, so the BIV has as few moving parts as possible to help avoid problems.

MOON REGAN
TRANSANTARCTIC
EXPEDITION

www.earthl

Design · RT

Earthly Ene

UNIVERSAL
RACING
SERVICES

Imperial College
London

www.transantarcticexpedition

Three-blade, variable-pitched propellor is powered by a Rotax 914 aircraft engine, run on biodiesel. The Rotax is well suited to high altitudes and low temperatures.

BIO-INSPIRED ICE VEHICLE

WHEN	2012
HOW HEAVY	700 KG
TOP SPEED	135 KM/H
SIZE	4.5 M LONG

MAKING TRACKS

Polar vehicles usually have tracks rather than skis. The tracks make it easier to go uphill and over difficult ground, but make the vehicles much heavier as they need a more powerful motor.

SKIDOO!

Snowmobiles have a track at the back and skis at the front. Most have a four-stroke engine producing 110 kW or more, and tracks made of Kevlar. Some are used as emergency vehicles, and by people who work in the snow, such as reindeer herders. Others are sports vehicles. Racing snowmobiles can reach speeds of 240 km/h and dragster snowmobiles up to 320 km/h.

Snowmobiles can be raced on snow, but also on grass.

SAFETY FIRST

The BIV goes ahead of two science support vehicles, finding a safe route. It uses cameras and ground-penetrating radar to investigate the ground and highly sensitive GPS systems to track its location. It also has sensors to monitor the driver's body so that it can pick up any problems such as the start of hypothermia. The information is sent wirelessly to a computer on one of the science support vehicles for instant analysis.

STON WONG
Dunkirk Garage
SPIRED VEHICLE

Three skis with independent suspension for gliding over the snow, and a spiked snow brake to stop safely.

SLOWEST CRAWLER

NASA CRAWLER

This giant crawler is used to move Space Shuttles to the launch sites. It's as wide as a six-lane highway and, carrying a rocket, as tall as a skyscraper. The crawler is too heavy for normal roads – it would destroy the road surface.

The Space Shuttles make their final journey, or roll-out, to the launch pad already fitted to their mobile launcher. The trip of just under 5.5 km takes six hours as it has to go so carefully and slowly.

Tiny steering wheel – the size of the steering wheel in a go-kart. Hydraulics enable it to turn the gigantic crawler.

3 SIDE

Two giant belts at each corner have 57 shoes (456 in total), each nearly 2.3 m tall, 0.5 m wide and weighing almost a tonne.

PRECISION WORK

Hydraulics move the platform to the right level to shift the spacecraft from its support pedestals onto the crawler, and from the crawler onto the launch tower. It takes 30 minutes to move the platform up to receive the Shuttle. The hardest part is driving it up a ramp to the launch position. The crawler uses precision laser equipment to get the Shuttle in just the right place.

NASA CRAWLER

WHEN	1963
HOW HEAVY	2,495,000 KG; 8,000,000 KG (LOADED)
TOP SPEED	9.66 KM/H (BUT ROUTINE SPEED IS 1.6 KM/H)
SIZE	34.4 M WIDE 9.5 M LONG
FUEL CONSUMPTION	355 LITRES PER KM
POWER	2 x 2023 KW ENGINES

A house on the road in 1940s America.

MOVING HOUSE

Nothing is as big as the crawler - but large vehicles have been used to move enormous loads since the invention of the truck.

Front and rear driver cabs and on-board bathroom and kitchen facilities for staff who take 14 hours to load, move and unload the Shuttle.

WEIGHT LIFTER

Carrying a Shuttle and launcher or a rocket, the crawler weighs a massive eight million kilograms. That takes a lot of power to move. Two diesel engines drive an electric motor that moves the crawler. One crawler is being upgraded to carry 8,165,000 kg so that it can move NASA's new heavy-lift rockets.

FASTEST PASSENGER TRAIN

CRH380A

The China Railways CRH380A is the fastest conventional train in the world. It runs on rails, unlike the faster maglev trains (pages 58-59) and hurtles between cities at up to 380 km/h.

The compartments are carefully constructed to reduce noise, and to keep air pressure inside stable even at very high speeds. New sound-absorbing and insulating materials were developed specially for use in the train and a new suspension design makes vibration almost zero.

Sleek, rotating paraboloid wedge structure designed to cut air resistance and reduce energy consumption.

Safe bogies can withstand speeds of 550 km/h without damage – much faster than the train's top speed.

⚙ ENERGY FROM STOPPING

The CRH380A has an electo-pneumatic regenerative braking system. This means that the energy of the train moving forwards is captured when it brakes and fed back in to power the train. It can achieve a feedback rate of 95%.

CRH380A

WHEN	2010
TOP SPEED	380 KM/H TOP OPERATING SPEED; 416.6 KM/H FASTEST EVER
ACCELERATION	0-380 KM/H IN 7 MINUTES
SIZE	203 M LONG
POWER	9,600 KW

Lightweight aluminium-alloy body that is highly pressurised to keep the pressure stable inside.

⚙ FASTER THAN A SPEEDING BULLET?

The Japanese bullet trains run at up to 300 km/h, connecting all the main cities in Japan. They run on special railway lines with only long, open curves and no tight corners so that the trains don't have to slow down.
There are nearly 2,400 km of high-speed track, making up the world's busiest high-speed rail network.

⚙ BOGIES

The body of a railway carriage is mounted on a **bogie** - a truck with special flanged wheels that fit onto a track. Because the raised part of the track fits into a groove in the wheels, it's hard for a train to be derailed. Suspension between the bogie and the carriage absorbs shock and vibration, making the ride more comfortable and protecting the carriage from damage.

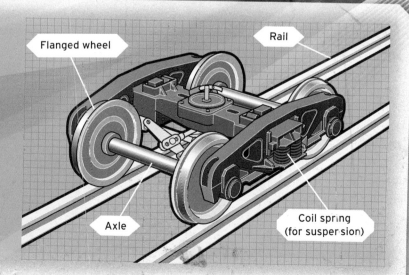

Flanged wheel

Rail

Axle

Coil spring (for suspension)

LONGEST TRAIN JOURNEY

TRANS-SIBERIAN RAILWAY

The longest single train journey in the world, without changing trains, is the Trans-Siberan Railway's service from Moscow in Russia to P'yongyang in North Korea. The weekly train takes 210 hours (nine days) to make the trip, a distance of 10,175 km.

Both passenger and freight trains run on the Trans-Siberian routes. Some freight trains are over a kilometre long, with 71 wagons and weighing 6,000 tonnes. Trains have 24 crew changes and four changes of locomotive on the journey.

Trains are designed to operate in temperatures of -40°c to +40°C.

⚙ SUPER-DUPER OPTION

Trips on the Trans-Siberian route are generally a few hundred pounds, but the special Golden Eagle from Moscow to Beijing costs up to £18,695! The train is pulled by the only remaining steam locomotive in Russia, and offers private suites with bathrooms, luxury restaurants and comfortable lounges.

There are other luxury trains, too. The Venice-Simplon Orient Express that runs between Paris in France and Venice, Italy, has polished wood panelling, marble bathrooms and extravagant restaurants.

TRANS-SIBERIAN RAILWAY	
WHEN	STARTED 1891
TOP SPEED	120 KM/H
LENGTH	10,175 KM

⚙ SHORTEST TRIP

The shortest public railway line is 95 m long. Called Angels Flight, it carries passengers up a steep hill in the city of Los Angeles, USA. The Trans-Siberian route from Moscow to P'yongyang is more than 107,000 times as far!

It costs just 50 cents to ride the tiny Angels Flight railway.

Electric train with overhead pantograph.

Each carriage has a corridor and is divided into compartments. There are first- and second-class carriages, all heated in winter.

⚙ MARATHON JOURNEY

The longest Trans-Siberian route runs from Moscow in the west of Russia, then heads south east towards the border with Kazakhstan. It crosses southern Siberia, skirting along the north border of Mongolia and through the far east of Russia into North Korea.

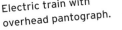

Moscow

RUSSIA

Novosibirsk

Irkutsk

KAZAKHSTAN

MONGOLIA

Khabarovsk

NORTH KOREA

P'yongyang

MIGHTIEST MAGLEV

SHANGHAI MAGLEV

The fastest maglev train service runs from Shanghai Pudong airport to the centre of Pudong. Its top operational speed is 431 km/h – faster than a Formula 1 racing car. The journey of 30.5 km takes only seven minutes and 20 seconds.

Maglev is short for 'magnetic **levitation**'. Maglev trains have no wheels, but are guided and propelled using a system of magnets in the guideway and the underside of the train. The train has three different systems: one for guidance, one for levitation and one for propulsion.

Inside the train, the ride is smooth and almost silent.

⚙ FASTEST EVER

The fastest speed ever recorded for any railed vehicle is 581 km/h, reached by the Japanese MLX01 maglev train. It uses wheels for support until it reaches a speed of 150 km/h because at low speeds the magnetic field is not strong enough for levitation. For its record-breaking run, it was configured as a three-car train, but can have a maximum of five cars.

The MLX01 running on Japan's Yamanash Maglev test line.

FLOATING

Strong magnets powered by electricity lift the train so that it floats a few centimetres above the guideway. With no moving parts in contact with the rails, there's no friction so the trains can go very fast. There is also no wear-and-tear so the trains last a long time.

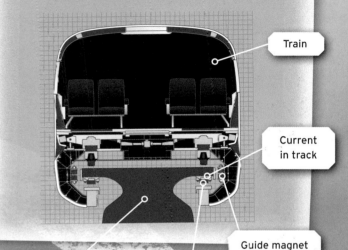

Train

Current in track

Guide magnet

Train magnet

Guideway

PUSHED AND PULLED

Magnetised coils of metal are embedded in the walls of the guideways. The polarity of the coils is switched very quickly to interact with magnets under the train. North and south poles attract each other but like poles (north/north and south/south) repel each other.

By alternately attracting and repelling magnets under the train, the train is both pushed and pulled forwards.

Train floats above the guideway, propelled and guided by strong magnetic fields.

Guideway raised above the ground and supported by giant columns every 25 m along the track.

SMT

TALLEST MONSTER TRUCK

BIGFOOT 5

Monster trucks are modified pickup trucks with custom suspension systems and giant wheels recycled from much larger vehicles. The Bigfoot 5 monster truck stands almost 5 m tall and was built specially to use its gigantic, ex-Army tyres.

Bigfoot 5 was first used for crushing cars in a publicity stunt. That attracted attention and more monster trucks followed. Now, monster trucks are often used for racing round obstacle courses, drag racing and mud driving as well as stunts.

Front and rear steering, with the rear steering driven by hydraulic pumps.

Eight 3-metre Firestone Tundra tyres weigh 1,088 kg each and were previously used on a US Army land train in Alaska.

Two truck frames make up the chassis that supports a modified body of a pickup truck.

BIGFOOT 5	
WHEN	1986
HOW HEAVY	12,700 KG
SIZE	5 M TALL
ENGINE	7.5 LITRE PETROL ENGINE

MONSTER DUMPER

The largest real dumper truck is the Liebherr T 282B. It's too big and heavy to drive on public roads, and is shipped in parts and built on site. It has a 90-litre diesel engine capable of generating 2,720 kW. The T 282B can haul a load of 363,000 kg and is used mostly in gold, copper, iron and coal mines in the USA, Chile, South Africa and Australia. Each truck costs around $5 million.

ALL CHANGE!

Most modern monster trucks have fibreglass body panels, which are easy and cheap to repair and much lighter than sheet metal. It's easy to switch fibreglass bodies quickly to change the identity of a truck. The body is a shell that covers the rest of the truck. It's sometimes moulded with a special customized design.

RUNNING AND JUMPING

Racing monster trucks often have the tyres shaved using special tools. Doing this, teams can create their own tread patterns, but can also cut the weight of the vehicle – they remove up to 90 kg from each tyre. In 1999, Bigfoot 14 made the longest monster truck jump ever, covering 61.6 m and clearing a Boeing 727 jetliner.

Monster trucks need good suspension to deal with jolts.

HEAVIEST HAULER

ROAD TRAIN

Road trains are chains of trailers pulled by enormous, powerful tractor units. The world record for the longest is held by a Mack Truck that pulled 112 trailers over 100 m in Clifton, Australia, in 2006.

Road trains are most common in Australia, Argentina and North America, where they are used to move livestock, fuel and ore dug from mines.

HOW TO LINK UP A ROAD TRAIN

The fifth wheel is a horseshoe-shaped flat metal plate with a gap for the kingpin (see below) to fit into. When positioned, the kingpin locks in place but can swivel within the fifth wheel. A flat plate covers the fifth wheel. The same mechanism is used to couple the prime mover and the first trailer, and between trailers.

The multi-wheeled trailers are self-tracking – they have steerable wheels at each end.

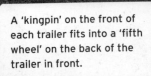

A 'kingpin' on the front of each trailer fits into a 'fifth wheel' on the back of the trailer in front.

BIGGEST HAULING TRUCK

The Liebherr T 282B is an off-highway truck for hauling powertrains (see right). It's a two-axle truck with a rigid frame and is diesel/electric powered. It can take a **payload** of 330,000 kg.

ALL IN A ROW

Most road trains have two to four trailers; those with five or six are called powertrains. Often, there's a second engine in the last trailer of the largest road trains, operated by remote control from the driver's cab. Without this help, the strain of pulling such weight can break the drive shaft of the prime mover, or unhitch the trailers.

In Australia, there's a weight limit of 115,000 kg and a length limit of 53.5 m for use on the roads. On private land, the legal limits don't apply and they can be real monsters!

The powerful truck at the front is the 'prime mover'. It has two drive axles and a single steer axle. It can be an articulated or rigid-bodied truck.

ROAD TRAIN	
LENGTH	1,474.3 M
WEIGHT	1,279 TONNES
PRIME MOVER	MACK TITAN

BIGGEST BORER

BERTHA

Tunnels are drilled by massive 'moles' called Tunnel Boring Machines (TBMs) – and the most massive of all is Bertha, built by Hitachi Zosen Corporation in Japan.

As Bertha moves along, vast cutting tools grind away at the earth in front of her. The muck is carried away, back along Bertha's length, to be dumped. As she clears a path, Bertha inches forwards very slowly. She moves at only 7.5 cm per minute - that's 756 m per week!

⚙ LASER GUIDANCE SYSTEM

Bertha is guided by laser. The laser is projected from behind the TBM and received by a guidance system at the front, precisely set to the planned path for the tunnel. The operator steers Bertha, adjusting the hydraulic arms with each push forward to align the machine correctly. Bertha should be able to get within 15 cm of her planned finishing point.

⚙ CUT TO SIZE

The cutting head at the front of Bertha is more than 17 m across and stands as tall as a six-storey building. That's just the very front of the machine - in total, Bertha is almost 100 m long. Bertha is shipped in 41 pieces. These are lowered by crane into an 80-m deep launch pit and put together underground.

⚙ LIFE IS BORING

Bertha operates 24 hours a day. Behind the drilling part of Bertha, a series of trailers holds bathrooms, a canteen, a control room, tool supplies and the electric motors that power the machinery. The power source is a local electricity substation.

393 cutting tools on the head chew their way through earth and rocks up to 120 cm across. Around 3.3 tonnes of metal are ground off the cutters for every kilometre of tunnel dug.

56 giant hydraulic arms adjust the cutting head until it's in position, while the main body is propped in place.

Behind the cutters, a massive corkscrew-like drill removes the muck – mostly earth and rocks – to a conveyor belt that carries it away.

BERTHA

WHEN	2013
HOW HEAVY	6,169,000 KG
SPEED	0.0045 KM/H
SIZE	17.4 M TALL; 99.4 M LONG
COST	$80,000,000

BIGGEST LAND VEHICLE

BAGGER 288

The gigantic Bagger 288 is one of a series of similar bucket-wheel excavators which vie for the title of largest land vehicle on Earth.

Instead of a single giant bucket, this type of excavator has a set of them arranged around a wheel. The buckets plough through the ground one after another as the wheel turns.

Bagger 288 can move 240,000 m³ of material a day. That's the equivalent of making a hole the size of a football pitch and 24 metres deep in a single day.

⚙ CRAWLER

The Bagger moves really slowly - it travelled at the rate of 1 km/h to reach the mine in Germany where it works. Moving the bucket-wheel and **counterweight** booms is very slow, too - depending on the direction, they might move only 5 m in a minute.

A massive boom acts as a counterweight to the bucket-wheel arm to stop the Bagger tipping over. The two are connected and controlled by cables.

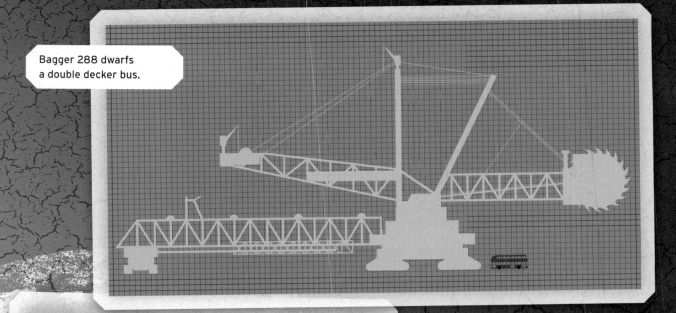

Bagger 288 dwarfs a double decker bus.

⚙ SENSITIVE SYSTEMS

The Bagger has five operators, but much of the work is automated with sensors, GPS, data acquisition systems and online monitoring. Sensors detect how much material is being moved and the speed of the conveyor belts is adjusted automatically. Managers and operators can track progress from data fed directly to the Internet.

BAGGER 288

WHEN	1978
HOW HEAVY	14,200,000 KG
TOP SPEED	1 KM/H
SIZE	220M LONG; 96M TALL

Each of the 20 buckets on the 23-m bucket-wheel can hold 5,500 m³ - about 80 bathtubs - of earth.

Earth and rubble are dropped through a chute onto a conveyor belt that takes them along the discharge boom to be dumped or spread on the ground.

TALLEST MOBILE CRANE

LIEBHERR LTM 11200-9.1

The tallest crane in the world is also the strongest. The Liebherr LTM 11200-9.1 could lift twelve blue whales at once. The boom uses hydraulics to extend up to 100 m. Unextended, it's as long as the truck and has to be transported separately between work sites.

The crane is used to lift heavy loads. One task it's particularly well suited to is installing and repairing huge wind turbines. These are too tall for most cranes to deal with, being about 100 m high.

Thick steel cables running up and over the boom hold the weight of the load.

The telescopic boom extends from 18.3 to 100 m using a hydraulic system. It takes nearly 13 minutes to extend from 50 m to its full 100 m.

The crane mechanism has its own six-cylinder turbodiesel engine that can deliver 240 kW.

LIEBHERR LTM 11200-9.1

WHEN	2007
WEIGHT	96,000 KG
TOP SPEED	75 KM/H
SIZE	20 M LONG; TALLEST REACH 100 M
POWER	500 KW

HELICOPTER HELP

Sometimes a load needs to be lifted higher than the tallest cranes can reach, or moved into a restricted space where a crane can't go. Then helicopters can be used instead, lifting and delivering a load.

A Boeing 747 Chinook helicopter lifts a vehicle.

DON'T FALL!

Huge bracing legs, called outriggers, extend sideways to create a wide, stable base for the superstructure. But this still would not be enough when the crane is holding a heavy load. It uses counterweights to prevent the load and the boom being heavier than the truck, and so tipping it over. It can take counterweights up to 202,000 kg.

TALLER STILL

The tower cranes used to build very tall buildings are even taller than the Liebherr LTM 11200-9.1, but they can't move around. They are built on a concrete base and have to be constructed on site. A tower crane has a tall tower, then a horizontal jib that carrries the load at one end and a counterweight - usually concrete slabs - at the other end.

BIGGEST DUMP TRUCK

CATERPILLAR 797F

The Caterpillar 797F is the world's biggest dump truck, capable of carrying more than 360,000 kg of rock and soil. These trucks are called ultra-class haulers.

The 797F is often used at mining sites where up to 81,000 kg can be dragged from the ground at a single shovel pass. Using such a big dumper truck saves money, as fewer trips are needed to move the load from where it is dug from the ground.

CATERPILLAR 797F

WHEN	2009
HOW HEAVY	623,690 KG
TOP SPEED	68 KM/H
SIZE	15 m long; 15.7 M HIGH (WITH BODY RAISED)
POWER	2,828 KW
ENGINE	Cat C175-20 ACERT

The truck is so tall the driver needs a ladder to get up to the cab.

The engine is huge, with 20 cylinders arranged in a single V-block. It has four turbo-chargers sucking air into the engine to enable it to burn fuel more quickly.

TOO BIG TO MOVE

The 797F is so big that it's put together at the customer's site. It's too heavy and wide to drive on public roads. It takes 12-13 semi-truck trailers to move all the parts - with two trucks just for the tyres, and four for the body. Putting it together takes seven engineers working round-the-clock for 20 days. If it has to be moved between sites, it must be taken apart and rebuilt afterwards.

The projecting shelf protects the cab from stray bits of load.

CAT 797
513

MINING ON MOUNTAINS

Some mining work takes place at high altitudes where the air pressure is low. This is a problem for engines that need lots of air to burn fuel. The 797F engine can be adjusted to work at sites up to 4,877 m above sea level - that's half the height of Mount Everest!

The 797F uses six of the largest tyres in the world: Michelin 59/80R63 XDRs. They're each 4 m tall, weigh 5,300 kg and cost $42,500.

REMOTE-CONTROL TRUCKS

Some mines in Australia, the USA and Chile use small fleets of ultra-class haulers that are remote controlled, with no drivers. The vehicles use sophisticated GPS systems and a combination of radar sensors and cameras to move around, avoiding obstacles.

MOST AMPHIBIOUS VEHICLE

WATERCAR PYTHON

If you've ever wished you could just drive across a lake or river, the WaterCar Python is what you need. It's an awesome amphibious vehicle – a car on land and a speedboat on water!

Each Python is hand-built and the new owner can choose the Corvette engine they want. There is a Dominator jet to provide power on the water. The interior of the boat/car is styled like a powerboat, with captains' seats in the front and a bench seat in the back.

WATERCAR PYTHON	
HOW HEAVY	1,723 KG
TOP SPEED	96.5 KM/H ON WATER; 201 KM/H ON LAND
ACCELERATION	0-95 KM/H IN 4.5 SECONDS
SIZE	6.25 M LONG
COST	$200,000-$220,000

A rotor and jet are used to move the Python when it is in the water, in boat mode. On land, it uses a normal engine and wheels.

The two doors have a perfect seal so that they never let in water.

⚙ WATER SKIS WITH ENGINES

A jetski is a personal amphibious vehicle that's a cross between a powerboat and motorbike. The Kawasaki Ultra 300X is a sports jetski with a 1,500 cc supercharged engine. It can deliver 221 kW of power that a jet pump turns into super propulsion.

The compact Phibian covers distance at speed.

EMERGENCY AMPHIBIANS

The Gibbs Phibian is an amphibious search and rescue vehicle. The carbon-fibre vehicle can travel at 48 km/h over water. It changes between land and water use in under ten seconds, with the wheels retracting to reduce drag and the dual jet-propulsion engine taking over. The Phibian is designed for use in police work and in response to natural disasters such as floods and tsunami.

LIKE A DUKW IN WATER

The DUKW was originally designed as a military vehicle. Renovated DUKWs are now used for tourist trips, as rescue vehicles and sometimes by fishermen. It was the first vehicle to allow the driver to change the tyre pressure from the cab, making it easy to drive over roads and over soft sand on a beach.

In water, the wheels are raised to be in line with the body, giving the Python a smooth planing hull like a speedboat.

Tourist DUKWs are a bright sight in London, UK.

FASTEST RACER ON WATER

SPIRIT OF AUSTRALIA

The fastest thing on the water is a speed-boat built of wood and fibreglass in an Australian backyard. Ken Warby built Spirit of Australia in the 1970s and then piloted it himself, setting a world speed record of 511.11 km/h in 1978.

Spirit of Australia is powered by a Westinghouse J34 jet engine, originally designed for use in jet fighters and other planes in the late 1940s. Warby bought it secondhand at auction for $69.

⚙ FLOATING ON AIR

The fastest boats have two wide sponsons, a bit like fat skis, and a space between them. The boat glides over the water on the sponsons, with air rushing through the space and giving the boat lift. At high speed, the front lifts up, and just part of the sponson and the rudder stay in contact with the water.

⚙ IN CONTROL

Racing powerboats are used on lakes and rivers, but for speedboats used on the sea, navigation is important. The speedboat controls include a digital display of a map, showing the position of the boat. There aren't many landmarks at sea, so this is vital.

⚙ POWERBOAT RACING

Formula 1 powerboat racing is very like F1 car racing except that it's on water. The powerboats are optimised for speed, with powerful jet engines and streamlined shapes. They are tunnel-hull catamarans, with only a few centimetres of the boat in contact with the water at top speeds. F1 powerboats are super-light – 390 kg, of which around a third is the engine. They can reach top speeds of around 250 km/h.

The aerodynamic shape cuts drag. The boat is not built for turning, though – it only goes in a straight line!

The frame is made of spruce and oregon, with plywood and fibreglass covering, making it light and strong.

Spirit of Australia is a three-point hydroplane – the only parts to touch the water at top speed are the two front sponsons and the rudder at the back.

SPIRIT OF AUSTRALIA

WHEN	1978
HOW HEAVY	1,500 KG
TOP SPEED	511.11 KM/H
SIZE	8.22 M LONG
COST	$10,000
POWER	4,474 KW; 1,587 KG THRUST
ENGINE	WESTINGHOUSE J34

SMALLEST SUB

PERSONAL SUBMARINE

How would you like your own personal submarine? Several people have built their own. This one was made by Mikhail Puchkov in Ryazan, Russia. He built it secretly in his attic and tried it out in the middle of the night when no one could see.

Puchkov's submarine can travel at 7.4 km/h and can go from St Petersburg to an island near Finland and back without stopping. The trip is a total of 320 km.

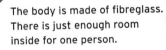

The body is made of fibreglass. There is just enough room inside for one person.

Originally only pedal-powered, the latest version of Puchkov's submarine has an engine for use on the surface and a different motor for underwater use.

⚙ PERSONAL DOLPHIN

People who don't want to build their own submarine can buy a personal submersible. One of the coolest must be the Dolphin Seabreacher - styled to look just like a dolphin! It can leap and even roll like a dolphin, and dive to 5 m for short periods. Each one is custom built - it can be very dolphin-like or disguised as a shark or whale.

The Dolphin can travel at up to 40km/h on the surface.

Tiny portholes allow the pilot to see out.

⚙ UNDERWATER CYCLING

The Omer-8 submarine is the latest in a line of person-powered submarines created by a student team in Montreal, Canada. The pilot cycles to drive the propellor which pushes the sub through the water. The propellor has a sophisticated electronic control system, though - it's more advanced than Puchkov's sub and can go at twice the speed.

⚙ DOWN WITH THE FISHES

Small submersibles are used by scientists and even tourists to watch fish in their natural environment. The Nemo 100 is a German mini-submarine that takes tourists on dives to see the underwater wildlife of the Baltic Sea.

PERSONAL SUBMARINE

WHEN	1988 (FIRST SUCCESSFUL DIVE)
TOP SPEED	7.4 KM/H
SIZE	14.8 M (MODEL WITH ENGINE); 3 M (MODEL WITHOUT ENGINE)

DEEPEST DIVER

KAIKO

The deep sea is very, very deep. But the Kaiko unmanned submersible has been there – 10,911 m down in the Challenger Deep, the deepest area of sea on Earth.

Kaiko had sonar scanners and four video cameras to film and map the ocean floor. The submersible was lost when the cable connecting it to its launcher broke during a typhoon in 2003.

⚙ WHAT'S DOWN THERE?

Unmanned submersibles are used for lots of purposes. Some carry scanners, cameras and radar to help map and investigate the ocean floor. Others collect samples of water, rock and wildlife from areas like deep sea trenches, which have some of the harshest environments on Earth. Automated submersibles also used to take fascinating films in the deep sea.

Unmanned submersibles can film deep-sunken wrecks.

KAIKO

WHEN	1995
HOW HEAVY	5,000 KG
SIZE	3 M LONG

Kaiko was connected by 250 m of cable to a launcher which itself had 12 km of towing, power and communication cables linking it to a support ship at the surface.

SUN POWER – UNDERWATER!

SAUV II is a solar-powered, unmanned submersible that can dive to 500 m. It has a 1 m² solar panel that charges a lithium ion battery. It's used for monitoring sea conditions, coastal surveillance and security, and even for tracking water quality in reservoirs. It's remotely controlled by computer, and sends back data using a wireless connection.

Mechanical manipulating arms worked to collect samples from the sea bed. The arms could handle a raw egg without breaking it.

DEEPEST MANNED DIVE

The deepest dive by a manned submersible was 10,911 m in the Challenger Deep trench in 1960 by the Trieste. Beaneath a 15 m long float chamber, it had a spherical cabin for a crew of two, with metal walls 12.7 cm thick to withstand 1,000 times atmospheric pressure. It took three hours and 15 minutes to descend to the ocean floor.

LONGEST SHIP

SEAWISE GIANT

The world's largest supertanker was Seawise Giant, an ultra-large crude carrier. It was powered by the largest diesel engine in the world. At its top speed of around 30 km/h it took 8.9 km to stop.

Although not quite the heaviest ship ever built, Seawise Giant was the longest. It worked transporting oil, but was bombed and sank during the Iran-Iraq war in 1988. It was salvaged and repaired and sailed until 2004. It then served as a floating oil storage container, but was scrapped in 2010.

The name of the ship changed several times. It was called Knock Nevis when it finally retired.

KNOCK NEVIS

The distance from the waterline to the bottom of the **keel** was 24.6 m, making it too big to navigate the Panama Canal or the English Channel.

⚙ BIG PARTS

Every bit of Seawise Giant was huge. The anchor alone weighed over 30,000 kg. The rudder weighed 208,000 kg and the propellor was 9 m across and weighed 45,000 kg. The displacement of the whole ship, when loaded, was 646,642,000 kg. The weight of a ship is given as the mass of water it displaces.

⚙ STEERING A GIANT

As the five-blade propellor of a ship like Seawise Giant turns, it creates both pushing and pulling forces on the water. The water is pulled into the turning propellor and forced out of the back, creating a jet effect which pushes the ship forwards. A rudder controls the direction the ship goes in. The flat blade of the rudder redirects the stream of water flowing round the hull and so turns the ship to the side.

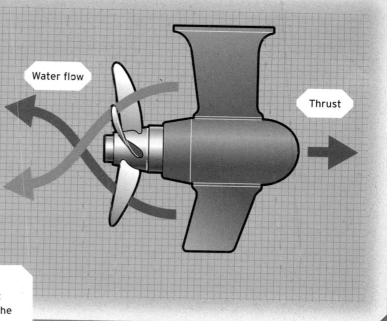

Water flow

Thrust

The propeller draws water in and forces it backwards, pushing the ship forwards.

Seawise Giant had 31,541 m² of deck space and over 46 tanks for holding crude oil.

The massive ship could carry more than half a billion kilograms of cargo, supplies and fuel – its so-called 'deadweight' capacity was 564,650,000 kg.

SEAWISE GIANT

WHEN	1981
HOW HEAVY	646,642,000 KG (LOADED DISPLACEMENT)
TOP SPEED (KPH)	30.6 KM/H
SIZE	458.45 M LONG
COST	$29,000,000
POWER	80,080 kW; 37300 KW

⚙ JUMBOISATION

Originally, Seawise Giant was going to be smaller. When the company that first ordered the ship cancelled the order, the hull was cut in half and an extra section added, making it longer – a process called 'jumboisation'. The company building it thought a bigger ship would be easier to sell.

FIRST FLYING HOVERCRAFT

19XRW HOVERWING

All hovercraft float on a cushion of air, but this hovercraft really flies! The 19XRW Hoverwing is a personal hovercraft with wings – a real cross between hovercraft and plane.

It can hover 28 cm above land or water on its vinyl-coated Nylon hover skirt - but with the wings fitted it can rise to 6 m and fly over rough terrain or choppy seas. It can also 'jump' up to 7 m to clear obstacles! With its twin-cylinder, turbocharged engine it can reach 126 km/h and travel for 225 km or four hours before refuelling.

⚙ FAST AND FLIGHTY

Formula 1 racing hovercraft are small, light personal hovercraft driven by a pilot on a track that is part land and part water. There are no restrictions on size or power in these races.

Removable wings convert the Hoverwing between a sleek hovercraft and a plane. The wings roll up to fit inside the Hoverwing while not in use.

Hovercraft racing is an increasingly popular sport.

19XRW HOVERWING	
WEIGHT	520 KG
TOP SPEED	126 KM/H
SIZE	5.8 M LONG; 2.3 M WIDE; 2 M TALL
COST	£150,000
POWER	176 KW

HOW A HOVERCRAFT WORKS

To move, the hovercraft has to lift off the ground and go forwards at the same time. An engine drives two fans. One of these inflates the skirt, making a cushion of air between the craft and the ground or water and lifting it. The other pushes air out of the back, providing thrust that drives the hovercraft forwards.

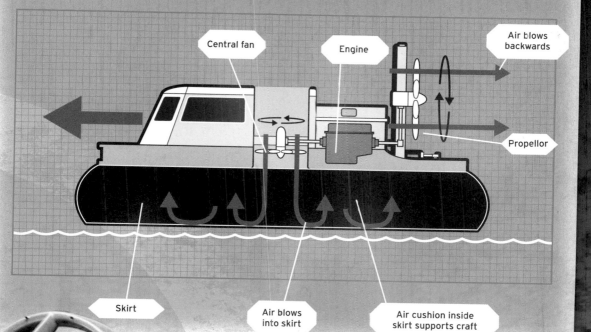

Central fan

Engine

Air blows backwards

Propellor

Skirt

Air blows into skirt

Air cushion inside skirt supports craft

A 1.5 m thrust propellor drives the hovercraft forwards, while an 86-cm, four-blade lift fan keeps it airborne (or skirt-borne).

The super-strong hull is made of Kevlar and carbon fibre over a lightweight foam core that provides positive floatation, making the Hoverwing unsinkable.

FASTEST HOVERER

The fastest hovercraft ever was specially streamlined Universal UH19P hovercraft called Jenny II. With Bob Windt as pilot, Jenny II reached 137.4 km/h in the 1995 World Hovercraft Championships in Portugal. It had a V6 engine driving two fans, one at the rear propelling the hovercraft forwards, and one underneath, providing lift.

BIGGEST LINER

ALLURE & OASIS OF THE SEAS

Giant passenger liners are more than floating hotels – they can be like small towns that sail the oceans.

Sister ships Allure of the Seas and Oasis of the Seas are massive – they each carry 5,400 passengers (6,296 maximum) and have a crew of 2,384. At 362 m long, they are the largest liners in the world. Allure of the Seas is 50 mm longer than its sister ship Oasis of the Seas. Each hull alone weighs 49,000,000 kg. There are 18 lifeboats that each hold 370 people – enough for 6,660 people.

Three 20,000-kW thrusters under the stern use electric motors to drive 6-metre propellers. There are no rudders; the ship is steered by moving the angle of the propellers.

⚙ THIRSTY SHIPS

Both ships use 5,210 litres of fuel per engine per hour for the 16-cylinder engines and 3,910 litres for the 12-cylinder engines – a total of 9,120 litres an hour.

ALLURE OF THE SEAS

WHEN	2010
HOW HEAVY (KG)	90,700,000 KG (LOADED DISPLACEMENT)
TOP SPEED (KPH)	42 KM/H
SIZE	362 M LONG; 65 M WIDE; 72 M TALL
COST	$1.2 BILLION
POWER	97,020 KW

LUXURY ON THE WAVES

Each of the ships has a dance hall that extends to two decks, a theatre to seat an audience of 1,380, a skating rink and a shopping mall. But that's not all. There are a zip-line, a mini-golf course, five swimming pools, a gym, volleyball and basketball courts, theme parks, night clubs, a spa especially for teens, a carousel, a science lab for young people, karaoke and comedy clubs. There's even a living park with 12,000 plants and 56 trees!

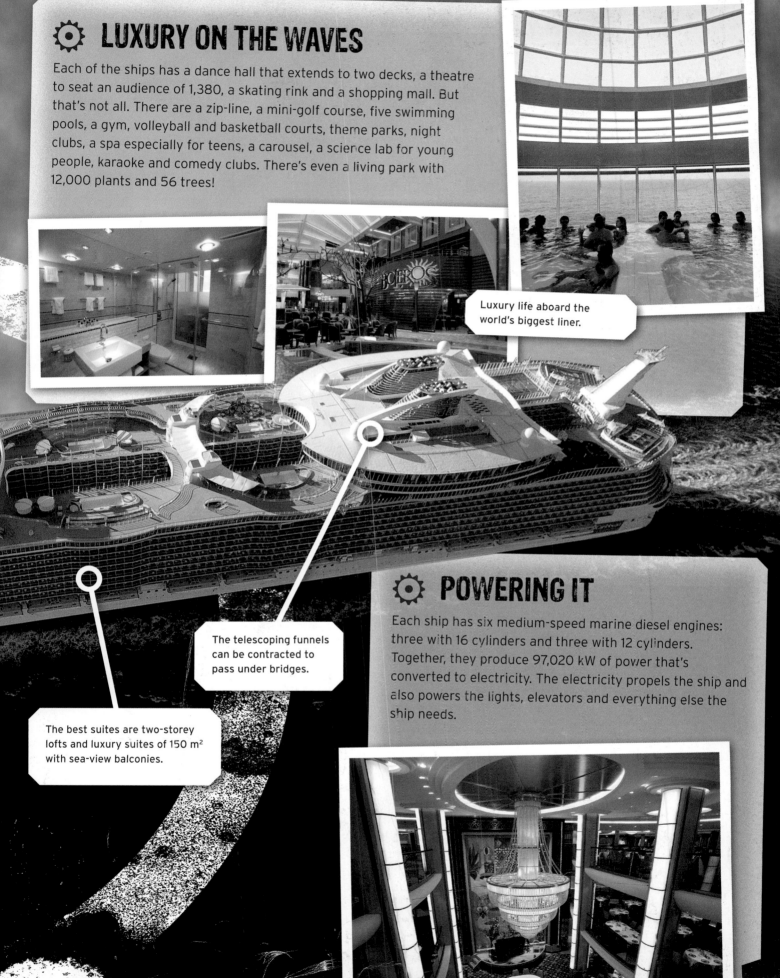

Luxury life aboard the world's biggest liner.

The telescoping funnels can be contracted to pass under bridges.

The best suites are two-storey lofts and luxury suites of 150 m² with sea-view balconies.

POWERING IT

Each ship has six medium-speed marine diesel engines: three with 16 cylinders and three with 12 cylinders. Together, they produce 97,020 kW of power that's converted to electricity. The electricity propels the ship and also powers the lights, elevators and everything else the ship needs.

85

ROUND-THE-WORLD RECORD BREAKER

EARTHRACE

The record for the fastest motorized boat to go all round the world is held by the strange-looking Earthrace. In 2008, it circled the globe in 60 days, 23 hours and 49 minutes.

The trimaran ran on bio-diesel and had other ecological features such as vegetable oil **lubricants**, **bilge-water** filters and composite materials made from hemp. It was used in anti-whaling operations, but sank in 2010 after colliding with a whaling support ship.

Twin propellors are mounted under the main hull and rudders are on the outriggers.

The trimaran design makes it harder to capsize and means it can go into shallower water than a monohull as it doesn't need a deep, weighted keel.

BIGGEST UNDER THE SUN

The Tûranor PlanetSolar became the first electric solar-powered vehicle to circle the globe in 2012 – it took 584 days. Its solar panels are capable of producing 93 kW of electricity to drive two motors. It can reach a maximum speed of 26 km/h, but its cruising speed is 13.9 km/h. At 31 m long and with displacement of 85,000 kg it can carry 200 people.

The Tûranor PlanetSolar has 500 m² of solar panels with 38,000 photovoltaic cells.

The vessel has space for 200 passengers.

EARTHRACE

WHEN	2008
TOP SPEED	59.3 KM/H
SIZE	24 M LONG; 7 M WIDE
COST	$2.5 MILLION
POWER	800 KW

A trimaran has a main hull and two outriggers attached to the main body of the boat by struts. Trimarans were first made by Polynesian islanders 4,000 years ago.

UNDERWATER BOAT

Earthrace was fully submersible. It could slice through 15-metre high waves and dive 7 m underwater. The hull was made of a composite of carbon fibre and Kevlar and coated with special, non-toxic, anti-fouling paint that prevents algae and marine creatures growing on it.

ROUND THE WORLD

Boats sailing around the world have a limited choice of routes. Unless they want to make long detours, they have to go through the Panama Canal that runs between North and South America, and through the Suez Canal in Egypt that joins the Red Sea and the Mediterranean.

SMALLEST JET FLIER

JETWING

The idea of a personal jet pack is very exciting – it's been in comics and movies for years. The JetWing personal flier is getting close. With a wingspan of just 2.4 m it's the smallest jet flier in the world.

The wing was designed by the Swiss pilot Yves Rossy. He has to launch himself from a helicopter or hot-air balloon and land by parachute. The only controls are a grip throttle to control speed and an altimeter that speaks the altitude. Rossy crossed the Grand Canyon and the English Channel using JetWing.

The wing and its jet engines fix onto the pilot's back with straps around the shoulders, chest, waist and thighs. The pilot steers by moving his head and body to shift his weight.

JUST LIKE FLASH GORDON

NASA developed the Manned Maneuvering Unit jet pack in the 1980s for use by astronauts outside a spacecraft. A real jet pack, like a superhero uses, is still some way off. In space, only a little thrust is needed to move a human, but on Earth a great deal of power would be needed from the jet pack.

The force from the jet pack is clearly visible over water.

POWERED PARACHUTES

Powered paragliding, or paramotoring, uses a parachute and a small motor strapped to the pilot's back. Paragliders can take off from the ground. They usually cruise at 25-70 kph and can reach up to 5,400 m. The pilot sits on a small seat that hangs from the paraglider wing, with the motor behind the seat. There are brake toggles and a throttle for control.

The pilot has to wear fireproof clothing as protection from the exhaust from the jet engines. Carbon-fibre heat shields on the jet nozzles give extra protection.

Four small Jet-Cat P200 jet engines under the wing are modified kerosene-fuelled model-aeroplane engines. The pilot carries 30 litres of fuel.

JETWING

HOW HEAVY	54 KG
TOP SPEED (KPH)	209 KM/H
SIZE	2.4 M WINGSPAN

TINY PLANE

The Bede BD-5 was an ultralight real aircraft sold in kit form in the 1970s. With a single seat and wingspan of 4.26-6.55 m, there were several versions including a jet-powered one, the BD-5J, which could reach 480 km/h. A Bede BD-5J featured in the James Bond film Octopussy.

LARGEST WINGSPAN

SPRUCE GOOSE

The Hughes H-4 Hercules Spruce Goose had a wingspan of an amazing 97.54 m, making it the largest ever to fly. It was also the largest-ever flying boat. It was a prototype and the only one ever built.

Because of war-time restrictions on the use of aluminium when it was built, the Spruce Goose was made mostly from wood. It could carry 750 soldiers, with all their equipment, or a single tank.

⚙ BIG WINGS, NO ENGINE

Gliders have a very large wingspan with a small, light body. As they have no engine, they depend entirely on lift from the air beneath their huge wings. The wings are very long and narrow, as this is the best aspect ratio for maximising lift and reducing drag.

SPRUCE GOOSE	
WHEN	1947
HOW HEAVY	180,000 KG (LOADED)
TOP SPEED	408 KM/H (CRUISE SPEED, NOT TOP SPEED)
SIZE	66.65 M LONG; 24.18 M WIDE
POWER	21,120 KW

⚙ WIDE, NOT LONG

The Goose was designed to carry troops across the Atlantic during the Second World War, but was completed in 1947 after the war ended. It made a single test flight, then never flew again, although it was maintained in flying condition until 1976. It remains the plane with the largest-ever wingspan, but modern jumbo jets are longer.

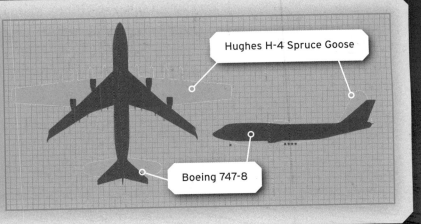

Hughes H-4 Spruce Goose

Boeing 747-8

The **fuselage** and wings were made from a wood-and-resin composite; the rudder and **elevators** were covered with fabric.

Each wing had four Pratt & Whitney R-4360 Wasp Major radial engines, each with a single four-blade propellor.

The fuselage had a single, large space with no windows for carrying troops and equipment.

⚙ TINY WINGS

The wingspan of the Stits Baby Bird is only 1.93 m. It's a high-wing monoplane with space for the pilot only. At 3.35 m long and weighing 114.3 kg, it has a maximum speed of 177 km/h and can climb to 2,880 m. The fuselage is made of steel tubing and the wings of wood.

LARGEST POWERED AIRSHIP

BULLET 580

At 71.6 m long, Bullet 580 is the largest inflatable powered airship. It can carry a load of 907 kg up to a height of 6 km.

This gigantic balloon took six hours to inflate. It can be flown by a crew or remotely controlled. Despite its size, it can operate from a small area as it takes off and lands vertically. The top speed is 129 km/h, but it doesn't have to go fast – it can hover over the same spot for up to a week!

The engine (not visible) runs on bio-fuel made from algae.

The outer envelope is made of Kevlar and is just over 1.5 mm thick, but it's ten times stronger than steel. If it has a hard landing, the balloon should just bounce!

⚙ BLIMPS AND RIGID AIRSHIPS

Airships can be non-rigid (a floppy skin that is inflated like a regular balloon), semi-rigid, or rigid. A semi-rigid airship has a solid framework but a floppy **envelope**. A rigid airship has a rigid envelope. Early rigid airships were made of canvas stretched over a wooden frame and then stiffened and made waterproof with resin. Blimps are non-rigid airships, like a giant balloon.

BULLET 580	
WHEN	2013
TOP SPEED	129 KM/H
SIZE	71.6 M LONG; 19.8 M DIAMETER – ABOUT 22,000M³
COST	$8,275,000

> The horrific Hindenburg disaster stopped people from wanting to travel by airship.

⚙ BIGGER, BUT NOT BETTER

An even larger airship, but rigid-bodied, was the German airship Hindenburg. It was the last of the great airships of the early twentieth century. The Hindenburg burst into flames when landing in 1937, killing 37 people. Early airships, including Hindenburg, were filled with hydrogen. It is lighter than the helium used now, but highly inflammable.

> Lift is provided by seven vast internal bags of helium, a gas lighter than air but that can't burn in an accident.

⚙ EARLY BALLOONS

Hot-air balloons were the first vehicles to take to the skies. Normal air was heated inside a balloon-shaped envelope by a fire. The pilot and passengers stood in a basket suspended beneath the balloon. The first flight was made in Paris by the Montgolfier brothers in 1783. In 1852, another French engineer, Henri Giffard, flew the first steam-powered airship.

FIRST FLYING CAR

TERRAFUGIA TRANSITION

Have you ever wanted a flying car? This is it! The Terrafugia Transition is a car-plane – it can fly like a car, then fold away its wings on landing and drive along the road just like a normal car.

When the Terrafugia switches between car and plane modes, the engine changes from driving the wheels to driving a push propeller at the rear of the plane. It's equipped with an airframe parachute – a parchute that supports the whole plane if there is a failure.

⚙ WHIRLY-CAR

The PAL-V One is a cross between a car, a motorbike and a gyrocopter. Its blades, propellor and tail all fold away to create an odd-looking three-wheeled vehicle that can drive on any road. Powered by a 160-kW aircraft engine, it can reach 180 km/h both on land and in the air. It's designed to fly at under 1,200 m so that it doesn't compete for airspace with commercial flights.

The PAL-V's rotors fold out of the way for road driving.

The cockpit has a light polycarbonate windscreen and windows to resist bird-strikes when flying, and modified airbags for safety on the road.

⚙ PARACHUTING CAR

The Parajet Skycar (in development) will combine a buggy-style road vehicle with a parachute. Driven by a 104-kW rotary engine, it can take off from a 200 m run of road or runway. It can fly at a maximum altitude of 4 km above sea level. On land, it's road legal but can also plough through sand and over rough terrain, with a top speed of 225 km/h.

The Skycar uses a custom-made paraglider wing.

⚙ GYROCOPTER OR HELICOPTER?

A helicopter has a powered rotor on the top. If the engine fails, the rotor stops. A gyrocopter has a powered propellor at the rear but the rotor blades are turned by moving air. If the engine fails, the gyro-blades keep turning and the craft can glide to Earth.

Electro-mechanical folding of the wings takes only 90 seconds and is triggered by a button inside the car/plane.

The wings fold at two points – upwards near the body and downwards mid-wing – so that they stow neatly.

TERRAFUGIA TRANSITION

WHEN	NOT YET RELEASED
HOW HEAVY (KG)	440
TOP SPEED (KPH)	185 KM/H IN AIR; 110 KM/H ON THE ROAD
FUEL CONSUMPTION	11 LITRES/100 KM (FLYING) 6.7 LITRES/100 KM (ON ROAD)
SIZE	8 M WINGSPAN; 2.3 M WIDE WITH WINGS FOLDED; 6 M LONG
COST	$279,000
POWER	75 KW
ENGINE	ROTAX 912ULS

SNEAKIEST SPYPLANE

NANO HUMMINGBIRD

Is it a bird? Is it a plane? It's both! The Nano Hummingbird is a drone – an unmanned aerial vehicle (UAV) used for surveillance. But it's cunningly disguised as a hummingbird to help it go unnoticed.

The Nano moves just like a real hummingbird: it flaps its wings and can hover, even in a gust of wind. It climbs and descends vertically, can fly forwards, backwards and sideways (left and right), and rotate clockwise and anti-clockwise. It can even fly through a doorway and send video from inside a building.

⚙ SELF-CONTROL

The Nano is controlled remotely by a pilot, sometimes working only from the video feed from the drone's camera. Other drones are autonomous, with onboard computers making decisions about where to go and what to do.

The body can be coloured to match real hummingbirds local to the area where the Nano is being used.

It's the same size and shape as a real hummingbird – larger than most species, but smaller than the largest real hummingbirds.

A tiny camera is hidden in the underside of the Nano and sends a live video feed to the remote pilot.

WHO'S LOOKING?

Military drones spy on enemies, but there are lots of other uses. In some countries, police use drones to monitor traffic, watch borders and look out for smugglers and pirates.

Drones are used for security over large areas (such as farms), and for checking the safety of oil pipelines that run over deserts.

They can even be used in search-and-rescue missions, searching for people lost at sea or in mountains.

DRONING ON

Some drones use different types of sensors, not just cameras. They can be used to detect levels of chemicals to monitor pollution, to check windspeeds around hurricanes, to search for underground oil or mineral deposits and even to track the movements of tagged animals.

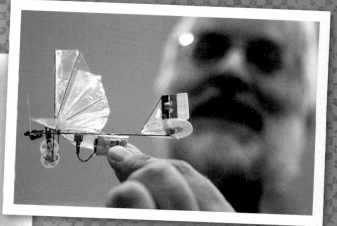

NANO HUMMINGBIRD	
WHEN	2011
HOW HEAVY	19 G (0.019 KG)
TOP SPEED	18 KM/H
SIZE	16 CM WINGSPAN

The BBC penguin-cam slides over ice to sneak up on birds!

BIGGEST HELICOPTER

MIL MI-26 HELICOPTER

The Russian Mil Mi-26 is a real monster of a helicopter. It's the largest and most powerful helicopter ever to go into production.

It can carry loads up to 20,000 kg, can fly at altitudes up to 4,600 m and has a range of 1,952 km. If the load is too bulky to fit in the hull, it is suspended beneath the helicopter with cables.

Two turboshaft engines mounted over the cockpit power the propellor. The blades can carry on working even if one engine fails (depending on the load).

Each of the eight rotor blades is 16 m long – the diameter of the blades is larger than the wingspan of a Boeing 737.

Using steel cables, and sometimes a sling, the helicopter can transport items too large to fit in the hull. Closed circuit TV lets the pilot monitor the load.

⚙ PLENTY OF ROOM INSIDE

The giant hull of the Mil has a cargo bay that can take tanks and other vehicles, or up to 80 people for troop movements or medical evacuations. Two electric winches on overhead rails can move loads along the cabin. Each is capable of carrying 2,500 kg. The floor has tie-down rings for securing loads.

⚙ MAMMOTH CARRYING A MAMMOTH

In 1999, a Mi-26 was used to transport a massive block of ice containing the frozen remains of an extinct Siberian mammoth, over 20,000 years old, to a science lab. The ice block weighed nearly 23,000 kg. The helicopter had to be returned to the factory and checked for damage immediately after the mission as the frozen mammoth was over the weight limit for lifting.

⚙ SMALL HOVERER

The tiny Hummingbird hover platform is just 2.2 m across. It has four small internal combustion engines capable of running the vehicle at up to 74 km/h. With a maximum hover height of 1,500 m, it can stay in the air for up to 30 minutes. The operator stands up, guiding the vehicle by shifting his or her weight. The Hummingbird is sold as a kit and takes 250 hours to build.

The pilot has to stand up for the ride on the platform.

MIL MI-26 HELICOPTER

WHEN	1977
HOW HEAVY	28,200 KG
TOP SPEED	295 KM/H
SIZE	40 M LONG, 32 M ROTOR DIAMETER
POWER	16,740 KW

SMALLEST PERSON-CARRYING VEHICLE

SOLOWHEEL

You can't get much smaller than a single wheel! The Solowheel is just that - one wheel with pedals to stand on and a small electric motor to drive it along.

The rechargeable battery gives a range of 16 km and a top speed of 16 km/h. To control acceleration, the rider leans forwards (to go faster) or backwards (to slow down or stop). Leaning to right or left controls the direction of travel. The Solowheel works as a gyroscope and is self-balancing once the wheel is spinning.

The rider controls direction and speed by leaning right, left, forwards or backwards.

SOLOWHEEL	
WEIGHT	11 KG (MAX LOAD 99 KG)
TOP SPEED	16 KM/H
SIZE	48 CM TALL; 20 CM THICK (PEDALS FOLDED)
COST	$1,795
POWER	1 KW

SEGWAY

The Segway PT (Personal Transporter) has two wheels, a platform to stand on and a handle to hold. It's much chunkier and less portable than the Solowheel, but can go further and tackle rougher terrain. The Segway has five sensors and two accelerometers to sense its angle with respect to gravity 100 times per second. It then applies motor torque to the wheels to rebalance, turn, accelerate or slow down as necessary.

GYRO-POWER

All self-balancing vehicles have a gyroscope at their heart. This comprises a spinning disc held inside a ring. If the disc is tilted as it spins (rotating the spin axis), the gyroscope adjusts by trying to tilt in the opposite direction to the force applied, so correcting its position. Three gyroscopes provide the autopilot system in a plane.

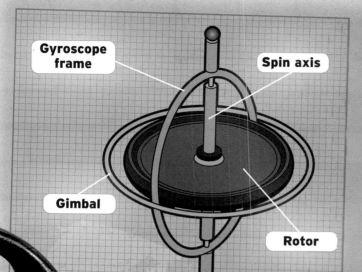

Gyroscope frame

Spin axis

Gimbal

Rotor

GYRO CAR

The Gyro-X was a prototype self-balancing car developed in California in 1967. With only two wheels and a gyroscope to maintain balance, the Gyro-X was the first – and last – of its kind, as the manufacturer went out of business before launching it. Despite its odd looks, the car could reach 200 km/h. While waiting three minutes for the 50-cm gyroscope to get up to speed, small outrigger wheels kept the car upright.

SOLOWHEEL

This two-wheeled car made a curious sight but never caught on.

A fold-down pedal each side of the wheel is all the rider has to balance on.

The wheel protrudes from the casing only at the very bottom, so clothing can't get caught in the wheel.

FASTEST FLIERS

NASA X-43A

NASA's hypersonic experimental X43 aircraft is the fastest thing in the air, capable of 10,461 km/h – ten times the speed of sound!

The X43 is an unmanned research craft, each one capable of only a single flight. It's launched from a B-52 carrier plane, on top of a winged booster rocket. The used rocket is discarded and the plane flies with its own hydrogen-powered **scramjet** engine, then crashes deliberately into the ocean after a short period of free flight.

The X-43 has onboard explosives that can be detonated remotely if anything goes wrong with the craft. The second of three X-43s was blown up in flight when it went off-course.

⚙ SCREAMING THROUGH THE AIR – MACH

Supersonic planes go faster than the speed of sound, Mach 1 (about 1,236 km/h at sea level). Hypersonic planes go faster than Mach 5. The scramjet engine in the X-43 can only operate at speeds faster than Mach 5 since it depends on very fast movement of the air-fuel mix through the engine.

The airframe on the X-43 is part of the propulsion system – air is drawn in through the front of the plane and expelled at the rear.

B-52

X-43

Booster rocket

U.S. AIR FORCE

ASTRO-PILOTS

The fastest piloted plane was the North American X-15, which reached 7,274 km/h in 1967. It also holds the record for the highest altitude for a manned plane, at 107.8 km in 1963. At this altitude, it was touching the edge of space, considered to be at 100 km!

Pilots flying the X-15 at altitudes of 80+ km count as astronauts!

WHY CRASH EXPERIMENTAL PLANES?

Most planes and engines are tested on the ground in wind tunnels. The movement of air around and through firstly models and later full-scale planes and parts is tracked and analysed by computer without the need for a flight. But wind tunnels can't reproduce the effects of hypersonic flight. The only way to test engines and plane designs at such speeds is to make them and fly them.

Carbon thermal protection material and circulating water protect the metal on the X-43 from melting as friction causes temperatures to reach nearly 2,000° Celsius.

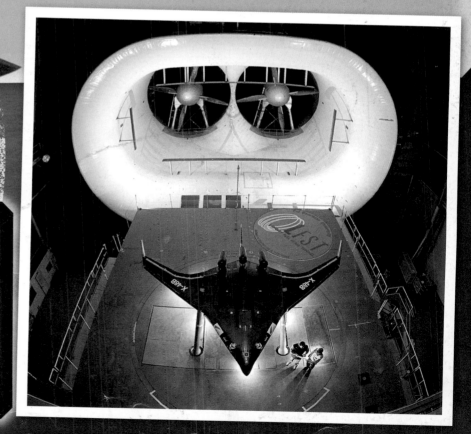

NASA X-43A

WHEN	2004
HOW HEAVY	1300 KG
TOP SPEED	10,461 KM/H
ALTITUDE	33,528 M
SIZE	3.7 M LONG

FURTHEST HUMAN-POWERED FLIGHT

MIT DAEDALUS 88

The MIT Daedalus 88 flew a record-breaking 115 km, powered by Olympic cyclist Kanellos Kanellopoulos. It took three hours, 54 minutes, 59 seconds – also setting the record for the longest human-powered flight.

The cyclist has to keep cycling all the time to keep the plane flying. The power from the pedals turns a drive shaft and goes through two gear boxes to turn the polystyrene propellor. Before take-off, the fragile wings must be supported by assistants running alongside the craft.

⚙ THE FIRST DAEDALUS

The flight was inspired by the mythical flight of Daedalus in ancient Greek myth. Daedalus and his son, Icarus, were imprisoned in Crete. Daedalus built them both sets of wings made from feathers, string and wax with which to escape. Icarus flew too high. The sun melted the wax and he fell to the sea and drowned, but Daedalus's flight was successful.

The frame and guide wires are made of Kevlar – a very tough and light material.

In myth, Daedalus was the first to try human-powered flight.

MIT DAEDALUS 88	
WHEN	1998
HOW HEAVY	31 KG
SIZE	8.6 M LONG; 34 M WINGSPAN

⚙ CROSSING THE CHANNEL

The first human-powered aircraft to cross the English Channel was the Gossamer Albatross, another cycle-powered plane, in 1979. It flew the 35.8 km in two hours and 49 minutes with a top speed of 29 km/h. Albatross's carbon-fibre frame is covered with Mylar and the wing ribs are polystyrene. It was the successor to the Gossamer Condor, the first ever successful human-powered plane.

The Albatross flew at an average of only 1.5 m above the sea.

The skin over the wings is made of Mylar – the stretched polyester film used for shiny helium party balloons. It's only 12.7 microns thick (a micron is a thousandth of a millimetre).

At 32 m, the wingspan of the Daedalus is larger than that of most Boeing 737s.

United Technologies

ΔΑΙΔΑΛΟΣ

DAEDALUS

⚙ FLAPPING WINGS

The first successful human-powered ornithopter is the Snowbird, though the first design for a flapping-wing plane was drawn up by Leonardo da Vinci in 1485! Snowbird has a wingspan of 32 m and is made mostly from carbon fibre, wood and foam.

LARGEST JUMBO JET

AIRBUS A380-800

The Airbus A380-800 is the largest jumbo jet in the world. It can carry 853 passengers over two floors. It has four jet engines, each producing 310,000-340,000 N of thrust depending on which engine type the client airline chooses.

It has a flying range of 15,700 km - far enough to go from New York to Hong Kong - which it can manage because it can carry 320,000 litres of fuel. It can fly up to 13,000 m - nearly 4 km higher than Mount Everest.

Together, the four engines use a litre of fuel every second.

QUALITY RIDE

Although the Airbus can take 853 people if all fly economy class, the seats can be moved to provide 521 seats in three classes, including an extravagant first class area. There can be seats that recline into beds and comfortable lounge and bar areas.

Quality or quantity? The Airbus is flexible.

PUTTING IT ALL TOGETHER

Large sections of the A380 are built in France, Germany, Spain and the UK. They are all moved to Toulouse in France by road, ferry and air. Smaller parts come from around the world. A network of ferries, adapted roads, canal barges and specially built port facilities was created to move the large components. The aircraft are assembled in Toulouse and flown to Hamburg for furnishing and painting.

It takes 3,600 litres of paint to cover the plane's surface, which has an area of 4,400 m². The paint alone weighs 500 kg!

There is 530 km of wiring used in the plane. The cabin has 98,000 separate wires and 40,000 connectors.

The landing gear has four main landing legs and a nose leg, with a total of 22 wheels.

AIRBUS A380-800	
HOW HEAVY	276,800 KG (EMPTY)
TOP SPEED	945 KM/H
SIZE	72.73 M LONG; 79.75 M WINGSPAN

JET ENGINES

The huge jet engines used in planes are also called gas turbines. A fan sucks air into the front of the engine. The air is compressed and mixed with fuel, and an electric spark sets light to the mixture. The burning gases blast from the back of the engine, so the engine and the aircraft are thrust forward.

The fan blades of the engine spin nearly 3,000 times a minute.

MOST POWERFUL ROCKET

SATURN V

The Saturn V rockets were the most powerful ever created. The first Saturn V launched Apollo 4 in 1967 and the last was used in 1973 to launch the Skylab space station.

The five rocket engines of the first stage started up 8.9 seconds before launch, firing 300 milliseconds apart. The engines burned 2,100,000 kg of rocket fuel in less than three minutes. If it had exploded on take-off, Saturn V would have generated as much energy as a small nuclear bomb.

SATURN V	
WHEN	1967
HOW HEAVY	2,800,000 KG (WITH FUEL) + PAYLOAD OF UP TO 120,000 KG
TOP SPEED	40,320 KM/H
SIZE	111 M LONG
POWER	34,500,000 NEWTONS OF THRUST

The five nozzles carry scorching-hot waste gases from the combustion chamber, blasting the rocket into space.

⚙ HOW SPACE ROCKETS WORK

In a rocket engine, the waste gases from burning fuel push the craft forward. On Earth, the fuel is mixed with air, but in space there is no air so the rocket has to carry oxygen. The fuel is converted to a gas and mixed with oxygen in the combustion chamber.

STAGED LAUNCH

As each stage burned its fuel, it separated from the rocket and the next stage fired. The first two stages fell away into the ocean; the last either hit the Moon or stayed in space. After establishing orbit, the stage 3 rockets fired again to push the craft towards the Moon, reaching a speed of 40,320 km/h. That's more than 11 km per second!

	Time burning	Speed	To altitude
Stage 1	2 minutes, 41 seconds	9,920 km/h	109 km
Stage 2	6 minutes	25,182 km/h	175 km
Stage 3	2 minutes, 30 seconds	28,054 km/h	191 km

The rocket had three stages, each with its own fuel supply – rocket fuel for the first stage, and liquid hydrogen for the other two.

Explosives fixed to the outside could be remotely detonated if anything went wrong.

The immense power of gases blasting from the engines forced the rocket up into the air.

Apollo spacecraft

Third stage

Second stage

First stage

MOST
INTREPID MOON
ROVER

LUNAKHOD

The Lunakhod Moon Rover was the first autonomous land vehicle to be used outside Earth. It was put on the Moon in 1970 by the Soviet space programme, taken there by Luna 17.

Lunakhod remained operational for 322 Earth days, making it the longest-lasting lunar rover. In that time it travelled 10.54 km, sent over 20,000 TV images back to Earth and tested the surface at 500 locations. NASA has located Lunakhod's position to within 1 cm.

Power for the rover was collected by solar cells on the underside of the lid during the two-week lunar day.

The eight wheels were each independently powered by electrical engines in sealed pressurised containers.

LUNAKHOD	
WHEN	1970
HOW HEAVY	840 KG
TOP SPEED	2 KM/H
SIZE	1.7 M LONG; 1.35 M HIGH

Eugene Cernan of the Apollo 17 mission drives the moon buggy on the Moon in 1972.

FIRST MANNED LUNAR ROVER

The Moon Buggy, or Lunar Roving Vehicle (LRV) developed by NASA was used on three Apollo Moon missions (15, 16 and 17). All three buggies are still on the Moon. Powered by a non-rechargeable 36-volt battery, the Moon Buggy had a range of 92 km. It had a frame of aluminium tubing, weighing a total of 210 kg on Earth (35 kg in the Moon's reduced gravity) and front- and rear-wheel drive to negotiate the difficult surface.

Antennae and four television cameras collected and transmitted film of the Moon's surface.

ROLLING, WALKING AND CLIMBING

NASA's Athlete robotic rover, which has not been used yet, has six wheels. It can roll over land like the Moon, or lock its wheels and 'walk' over very rough, sandy or steep ground. A new version in development will be able to climb vertical cliff-faces using a grappling hook. It can carry a payload of 300 kg (Earth mass) on its large, flat base.

FIRST SPACE-WALK PACK

MANNED MANOEUVRING UNIT

Astronauts don't just stay inside their spaceships all the time. For moving around in space - spacewalks - they can use jet-propelled packs called Manned Manoeuvring Units (MMU). The MMU was used in spacewalks on three missions in 1984.

The MMU had no engine, but used bursts of nitrogen, stored as a liquid and quickly turning to gas, to produce thrust, pushing the astronaut through space. The nitrogen escaped through one or more of 24 nozzles pointing in different directions.

UP, DOWN, LEFT, RIGHT AND ROUND AND ROUND

The astronaut used the left-hand controller to produce acceleration going forwards, backwards, up, down, left and right. The right-hand controller produced rotational acceleration to control roll, pitch, and yaw - the way a vehicle (or astronaut) turns around axes in three directions. The controls could be locked when the settings were right, leaving the astronaut's hands free for work.

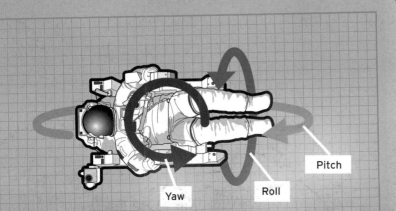

Yaw

Roll

Pitch

Twenty-four nozzles at different points around the pack produced thrust in different directions.

The unit fitted onto the astronaut's back, over the life-support system and the pressurised spacesuit.

MANNED MANOEUVRING UNIT

WHEN	1984
HOW HEAVY	148 KG (WITH FUEL)
TOP SPEED	87.84 KM/H

⚙ PIGGY-BACK PACK

The MMUs were stored on the wall near the airlock hatch, with the arms folded down. The astronaut had to back into the unit. When the life-support system snapped into place, the arms folded down.

Fingertip controllers for direction were on the end of the long 'arms'.
The length of these was adjustable to fit astronauts of different sizes.

A NASA astronaut tethered to a spacecraft.

⚙ MOVING IN SPACE

On Earth, a person or vehicle has to move against gravity, air resistance and friction against a surface.
In space, none of these constrains movement. Even a tiny force can move something a long way - the gravitational pull of the Earth, or pushing against something, can make an astronaut drift away. To prevent this, astronauts can be tethered to the spacecraft or use an MMU.

MOST
HARDWORKING
SPACECRAFT

DISCOVERY

The Space Shuttle Discovery completed 39 missions between 1984 and 2011. It travelled 238,539,663 km, orbiting the Earth 5,830 times. That makes it the hardest working of the five Space Shuttles.

Discovery launched with a giant tank of liquid fuel and two solid-fuel rocket boosters. The Shuttle's main engines drew hydrogen and oxygen from the main fuel tank. After two minutes, the used rocket boosters detached, parachuting into the ocean for recovery and re-use. Seven minutes later, the external fuel tank detached and burnt up in the atmosphere.

The crew compartment was home to the astronauts for up to two weeks. The flight deck was above, with the sleeping, storage and bathroom area beneath it.

⚙ SHUTTLE AT WORK

The Shuttles were used to deploy and retrieve satellites and to deliver astronauts and components to the International Space Station. A reaction control system (RCS) used 14 jets to nudge the Shuttle round to control its direction, using the same self-igniting fuel-mix as the OMS engines (see opposite). A remote manipulator arm that extended from the cargo section positioned and retrieved satellites.

DISCOVERY	
WHEN	1984-2011
HOW HEAVY	2,050,000 KG
TOP SPEED	27,875 KM/H
SIZE	23.7 M WINGSPAN; 56 M LONG

TELESCOPE IN SPACE

In 1990, Discovery carried the Hubble Space Telescope into orbit. Just 4.3 m across, it is a visible-light telescope that collects and sends to Earth crystal-clear images of the stars. Because it is outside Earth's atmosphere, there is no distortion or background light to interfere with the images.

The Orion nebula, photographed by the Hubble Space Telescope, is about 1,350 light years away and 24 light years across.

Discovery

Three main engines at the rear were each 4.3 m long, 2.3 m across the nozzle and 3,039 kg in weight. They burned mixed liquid hydrogen and oxygen.

Exhaust gases left the nozzles at 10,000 km/h. Each engine produced up to 2,090,664 N of thrust.

ENGINES IN ORBIT

Two orbital manoeuvring system (OMS) engines controlled the position of the Shuttle. Their rocket engines were powered by two gases which, mixed together, self-combusted with no spark necessary. Each engine could produce 26,000 N of force, could start and stop 1,000 times, and burn for a total of 15 hours.

To land, the Shuttle faced Earth and the engines fired it for the descent.

MOST RESILIENT MARS ROVER

OPPORTUNITY

Two rovers sent to Mars in 2003 landed in 2004 and set about exploring the surface of the planet, sending images and other data back to Earth. Originally intended to work for 92 days, one of them - Opportunity - was still operational nine years later in 2013.

Opportunity and its twin Spirit landed on Mars coccooned inside balloons and airbags and with a parachute to slow their descent. They were dropped from the Delta II rocket used to carry them to Mars, a journey that took 202 days. Opportunity is powered by solar panels and a rechargeable lithium-ion battery.

⚙ WORKING HARD

Opportunity has spent its time photographing the Martian landscape and collecting and examining samples of rock and soil. Its actions are controlled from Earth.

In 2006, the software controlling Opportunity was updated to enable it to make its own decisions about whether to photograph a scene and whether to collect a sample. This change cuts the amount of data sent between the rover and Earth.

Each wheel has its own motor. The rover has front and rear steering and can operate at an angle of 30°, so it can traverse slopes.

⚙ ROLL-OVER ROVER

A design for an unusual Mars rover is being investigated by NASA. The tumbleweed rovers would be blown around the planet by the Martian winds. One design has an internal network of sails; another looks like a giant balloon. The wind would carry the rovers to places too difficult to reach by other methods.

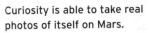
Curiosity is able to take real photos of itself on Mars.

The rover Curiosity, deployed in 2012, is the size of a car. Its mission includes looking for evidence that the landing area could once have supported life. In 2013 Curiosity found a stream bed with rounded pebbles, showing that water once flowed on Mars. Water is essential to all known life.

Antennae are used to contact mission control. It takes four to 21 minutes for a radio signal to reach Earth from Mars, depending on the positions of the two planets.

The arm has an abraision tool for exposing fresh rock, magnets to collect magnetic dust particles, **spectrometers** to investigate samples and a microscopic imager for taking close-up, high-resolution images.

DISCOVERY

WHEN	2004-PRESENT
HOW HEAVY	185 KG
TOP SPEED	0.18 KM/H (50 MM/S) (AVERAGE SPEED ABOUT 0.06 KM/H)
SIZE	1.6 M LONG; 2.3 M WIDE; 1.5 M HIGH
POWER	MAXIMUM 33 WATTS PER HOUR FROM SOLAR PANELS

FASTEST HUMAN TRIP

APOLLO 10

Three people have travelled at the fastest speed ever achieved by a human – the crew of Apollo 10, which reached 39,896 km/h in 1969.

Apollo 10 was the last of the practice flights for the Moon landing. It went into low orbit around the Moon, then the lunar module detached and descended to 14 km above the Moon's surface, but did not land. It travelled a total distance of 1,334,850.26 km in eight days, 23 minutes and 23 seconds.

The lunar module is on top of the three-stage Saturn V rocket. The whole rocket is 110 m tall.

The Apollo 10 crew (left to right): Eugene Cernan, Thomas P. Stafford, John W. Young.

APOLLO 10	
WHEN	1969
TOP SPEED	39,896 KHM/H
SIZE	110 M
POWER	33,350,000 NEWTONS OF THRUST
ENGINE	5 X F-1 ROCKET ENGINES

The launch escape system at the very top could blast the command module away from the rest of the rocket and parachute to safety if anything went wrong.

A Helios prototype being fitted into a rocket cone.

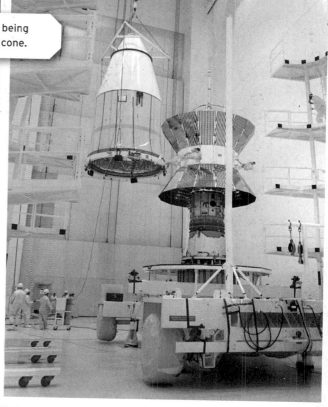

FASTEST FLIGHT

Although Apollo 10 was fast, the unmanned probe Helios 2 was even faster still, reaching a top speed of 252,792 km/h - 70.22 km/second - in April 1976.

Helios 1 and Helios 2 were launched in 1974 and 1976 to travel close to the Sun and collect data about cosmic rays, cosmic dust, solar plasma and solar winds. Helios 2 flew to within 0.29 AU of the Sun (about 43,500,000 km). The probes are still orbiting the Sun, but they no longer send data to Earth.

HOW TO GO REALLY FAST

Rockets work in the same way as jet engines - by producing thrust in the form of a burst of exhaust gas from the rear of a vehicle. In space, there is little gravity and no air resistance, so the same amount of thrust produces greater acceleration in space than on Earth..

Five F-1 rocket engines each 5.5 m long and capable of producing 6,670,000 N of thrust fire together to blast the rocket carrying Apollo 10 into space.

HOW TO CHEAT AND GO EVEN FASTER

Some spacecraft harness the gravitational field of a planet and use it as a sort of slingshot. This is called a gravity assist manoeuvre. The craft is pulled towards the planet by gravity, accelerating rapidly, then whizzes past, using the extra speed to accelerate into space.

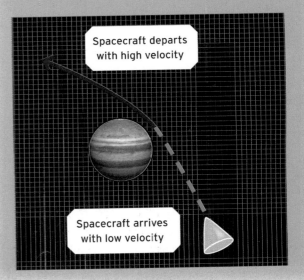

Spacecraft departs with high velocity

Spacecraft arrives with low velocity

FURTHEST TRAVELLING SPACE PROBE

VOYAGER 1

The most distant man-made object is the Voyager 1 probe, launched in 1977. It has travelled 18 billion km – it's at the edge of the Solar System and still going.

Voyagers 1 and 2 were launched to take advantage of an alignment of the planets that happens only once every 177 years and would enable Voyager 2 to visit Jupiter, Saturn, Uranus and Neptune in sequence.

Radioisotope thermoelectric generators produce electricity to run the instruments onboard Voyager, receive transmissions from Earth and send data back to Earth.

IS THERE ANYBODY OUT THERE?

Both Voyagers carry a gold disk and an instrument to play the disk, which holds 115 images of Earth, recordings of music from different times and places, and greetings spoken in 55 languages including Akkadian – last spoken 6,000 years ago. There is a diagram showing the location of our Sun and instructions on playing the disk which any advanced civilization could decode. A spot of uranium-238, which has a half-life of 4.51 billion years, will help any aliens work out when Voyager was made.

The Voyager disks are made of gold because it does not corrode.

Antennae for detecting radio and plasma waves.

VOYAGER I	
WHEN	1977–NOW
WEIGHT	773 KG
TOP SPEED	3.6 AU/YEAR; 61,600 KM/H
POWER	0.47 KW (AT LAUNCH)
ENGINE	3 X RADIOISOTOPE THERMOELECTRIC GENERATORS

Instruments for measuring and recording magnetic fields, solar wind and interstellar wind, detecting particles and cosmic rays and taking photographs.

POWERING THROUGH THE DARKNESS

The power for the Voyagers comes from the radioactive decay of plutonium-238, which has a half-life of 87.7 years. That and the deterioration of components means Voyagers now have only 57% of the power they had at launch. Power will run out in 2020, when Voyager 1 will be 20 billion km from the Sun. It will then drift.

A LONG PATH

Voyager 1 was launched slightly later than Voyager 2 and has visited fewer planets. It is further from Earth than Voyager 2 and travelling faster. It used a gravity-assist move from Saturn to boost its speed. It is heading out of the Solar System, into interstellar space, at the rate of 61,350 km/h. If it were heading for the nearest star (which it isn't), it would take 73,775 years to get there.

BIGGEST SPACECRAFT

THE INTERNATIONAL SPACE STATION

The largest human-made object in space is the International Space Station (ISS), started in 1998 and built up in a modular way from components carried by Space Shuttles and put together in space.

It's the ninth inhabited space station and the largest at 72 m long and weighing 450,000 kg. It's large enough to be seen with the naked eye from Earth. It has been permanently inhabited since November 2000. ISS is funded until 2020 and could stay in use until 2028.

The ISS is in orbit between 330 km and 410 km above Earth and completes 15.7 orbits each day.

Arrays of photovoltaic cells collect solar power for the ISS to use.

⚙ WORKING IN SPACE

The ISS provides laboratory facilities for carrying out experiments in microgravity and space conditions. These include work on astrobiology, astronomy, space medicine, physics, materials science and space weather. Space medicine studies the behaviour of the human body in space. It is essential to understand this before humans make long space flights or colonize other planets. Scientists also use a special detector to investigate mysterious dark matter. This could not be done anywhere else.

An astronaut conducts experiments aboard the ISS.

⚙ LIFE AWAY FROM HOME

Astronauts live on the ISS for months at a time. Sleep stations are scattered around the station. Crew wash with water jets and wipes, rather than showers. They eat packaged food, taking drinks and soup from bags with a straw. Knives and forks are held to metal trays with magnets to stop them floating away. Most food has sauce, to stop crumbs floating around.

INTERNATIONAL SPACE STATION	
WHEN	1998-PRESENT
WEIGHT	450,000 KG
TOP SPEED	27,743.8 KM/H
POWER	0.47 KW (AT LAUNCH)
SIZE	72.8 M LONG; 108.5 M WIDE; 20 M HIGH

⚙ GOING TO WORK

Astronauts and equipment are taken to the ISS by smaller spacecraft. Equipment and supplies are often ferried there in unmanned craft. Each craft has to dock with the ISS - a complex and precise manoeuvre. It involves the two vehicles colliding at an exact position, with giant springs absorbing the shock of the impact.

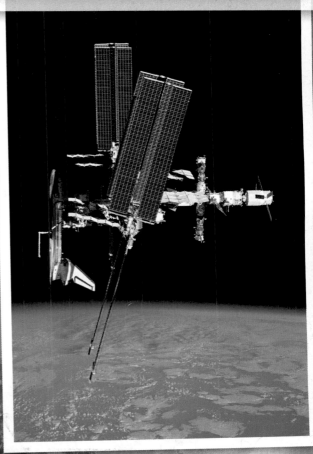

The ISS is made up of a set of modules containing laboratories, command modules, crew quarters, stores and equipment.

FIRST COMMERCIAL SPACECRAFT

SPACESHIP TWO

How would you like to fly into space? With the launch of SpaceShip Two, it will become possible. It's a suborbital plane, which means it flies at the upper edge of the atmosphere but below the altitude of the lowest orbiting bodies.

Produced for Virgin Galactic, SpaceShip Two is the first space vehicle to take paying passengers. It can carry six passengers and two crew members, who will experience microgravity for a few minutes of the two-and-a-half hour flight. Tickets cost from $200,000.

Wings pivot upwards to create a shape with maximum drag for re-entry. Then they fold downwards to allow the craft to glide to the runway.

SPACESHIP TWO	
WHEN	2013
TOP SPEED	4,200 KM/H
SIZE	8.23 M WINGSPAN; 18.29 M LONG

⚙ SOLID OR LIQUID?

Rocket engines can burn solid or liquid fuels. Liquid fuels are usually two gases in liquid form at high pressure, often hydrogen and oxygen. Burning can be controlled, but it's an expensive and complex system. Solid fuel rockets are simpler and cheaper, but they are like a firework - once lit, the engine can't be shut off. SpaceShip Two has a new kind of engine that uses a solid fuel, but a liquid oxidizer. It can be controlled by limiting the oxygen, but it is cheap and simple like a solid fuel system.

⚙ LIFT OFF!

SpaceShip Two is launched from the specially designed WhiteKnight Two. This looks like two planes joined together, with fuselages 15 m apart. SpaceShip Two fits between them, and is carried to an altitude of 15 km before being launched horizontally. SpaceShip Two then fires its rocket engine to get to its final altitude.
To descend, it folds up its wings and falls like a shuttlecock to 24 km, then folds down the wings and glides to land on a runway.

SpaceShip Two and its launch vehicle are made of carbon-fibre composite. It's four times as strong as steel and weighs only a quarter as much.

Windows overhead and to the side of each seat make sure that every passenger has a perfect view.

⚙ TOURISTS IN SPACE

Dennis Tito was the first-ever space tourist. He paid around $20 million to spend nearly eight days in space on the ISS. He flew with a Russian crew and carried out several experiments in space.

Dennis Tito was the first private visitor to the ISS.

MOST AWE-INSPIRING FUTURE VEHICLES

We've come a long way in the last 150 years. How far will we go in the next 150 years? Here are some of the vehicles that have been suggested or are in development.

A maintenance shaft (with air) is used by staff and in case of emergencies.

The shape of the Aeroscraft makes it a blimp-plane hybrid.

⚙ A NEW TYPE OF FLIGHT

The Aeroscraft is a giant airship of a completely new type: its lift is provided by both helium (like a blimp) and its shape (like an aeroplane). The largest model will be able to carry 453,000 kg – 500 times as much as the Bullet 580 (see pages 92-93). It could be used for passenger cruises lasting several days. It can take off and land vertically, using six downwards-facing, turbofan jet engines. In the air, it uses electric propellors at the rear to drive it forwards.

⚙ VACUUM TRAIN

A vacuum train (or vactrain) will travel through a sealed tube. If built, it could reach 6,400-8,000 km/h - 2 km per second! That's five to six times the speed of sound, but in the airless tube there would be no sonic boom. Using tunnels under the oceans, train travel could replace fights between the USA and Europe. It would take less than an hour to get from New York to London. Tubes could also be built on stilts above cities. In China, engineers are working on a first-stage vactrain that could travel at 1,000 km/h.

A vacuum train magnetically levitated from the track travels though a sealed airless tube. There is no air resistance, so the train can go very fast.

If the tunnel is under the sea, it is tethered to huge anchors to keep it in place. Above the surface, stilts are used.

⚙ ROBOT CARS

Cars that drive themselves have featured in movies for years. A team at Oxford University has created a prototype car controlled by an iPad. A laser scans the direction of travel 13 times a second. If the car detects an obstacle or a pedestrian, it brakes automatically. When the car is driven normally along a route, it uses lasers and cameras to scan and 'remember' the route. It can then repeat it automatically. The prototype is a modified Nissan Leaf. The navigation system costs only £5,000 – so the future may not be far away!

It may not look unusual, but this car drives itself!

GLOSSARY

Accumulator
In an hydraulic system, an accumulator is a storage reservoir in which fluid is held under pressure by, for example, a weight, a spring, or compressed gas.

Airbag
A fabric bag that inflates rapidly when a vehicle undergoes a collision. It cushions the driver and passengers, and prevents them from being injured by stopping them hitting objects such as the steering wheel.

Airbox
Motorbike engines suck air from their surroundings and into the airbox, which filters it before sending it to the engine.

Airbrake
Flaps that an aeroplane extends to increase drag during landing. They also feature on super-fast land vehicles such as the Bugatti Veyron.

Articulated
A vehicle with a pivoting joint that enables it to bend in the middle is said to be articulated. Articulation allows the vehicle to make sharper turns than would otherwise be possible.

Bilge-water
The bilge is the lowest part of a ship, where the two sides meet underneath. Water which drains from the deck through the ship ends up here, and becomes bilge-water. It has to be pumped out occasionally, or the ship will sink!

Bogie
A wheeled trolley that attaches to the main body of a vehicle such as a railway carriage. Bogies can be detachable, or fixed to carriages.

Chassis
A chassis (pronounced as 'shassi') is the internal framework which supports a vehicle. It functions in a similar way to the skeleton of an animal.

Counterweight
A weight that balances another weight. This can be useful in keeping large vehicles or objects steady – for example, in stopping a crane from toppling over.

Crankshaft
A shaft that turns the back-and-forth motion of the pistons of an engine into the rotary motion required to turn the wheels of a vehicle.

Differential
A device that splits an engine's torque two ways. Each output then spins at a different speed.

Drag
A force generated when a solid object pushes against a liquid or gas – for example, the rudder of a ship moving through water.

Electron
A subatomic particle (part of an atom) with a negative electric charge.

Elevator
Elevators on a plane are flaps that are used to control the pitch balance (the angle at which the plane is flying through the air).

Flybridge
The flybridge, or flying bridge, is an open area on top of a ship which gives a 360-degree view around the vessel.

Friction
Friction is the resistance that one surface or object meets when moving over another.

Fuselage
The fuselage is an aircraft's main body section. It carries passengers, cargo and crew.

Gyro-technology
Vehicles that are controlled by the driver leaning forwards or backwards, such as a Segway or the Uno, are said to use gyro-technology.

Hydraulics
The use of liquids as a medium to carry force from one part of a machine to another.

Hydrogen cell
A hydrogen cell converts chemical energy into electricity, producing only water as a waste product. Unlike a non-rechargeable battery, it can be refuelled.

Internal combustion engine
An engine that runs on a fuel such as petrol, combined with air. When a spark is applied, the fuel catches fire and the resulting energy drives the engine.

Ion
An atom or molecule that carries a positive or negative electric charge because it has lost or gained one or more electrons.

Keel
A blade sticking down into the water from the bottom of a boat. It prevents the boat from being blown sideways by the wind and holds ballast (heavy stuff) to keep the boat from overturning.

Kevlar
A tough and light synthetic fibre sometimes used in vehicle manufacture. It is made of short fibre filaments similar to Nylon.

Levitation
The process by which an object is suspended by a force such as magnetism.

Lubricant
A liquid introduced to reduce friction between moving surfaces. Most vehicle lubricants are oil-based.

Maglev
Magnetic levitation, or maglev, is a way of running trains without the use of wheels. Trains float above the guideway, propelled and guided by strong magnetic fields.

Monocoque
A monocoque (meaning 'single-shell') construction is one in which the outer skin is the load-bearing part of the structure. Early planes had an interior frame covered with a weak skin, but modern planes use a monocoque construction that requires no internal skeleton of struts.

Outrigger
A part of a boat or other vehicle that extends to the side of the main body. Outriggers are usually used to stop the vehicle from toppling over.

Payload
The total weight (of passengers and cargo) that a vehicle can carry.

Piezoelectricity
Electricity generated by certain solid materials, such as some crystals, when they are squeezed.

Piston
A piston is a cylinder fitted inside a tube. The tube also contains liquid or gas and when the fluid moves the piston moves with it. As the piston moves, it moves another component (such as a crankshaft), so transferring energy to another part of the engine.

Pneumatics
The use of a gas, usually air, to carry force from one part of a machine to another.

Ramjet
A kind of jet engine that uses the plane's forward motion to decelerate incoming air to subsonic speed and compress it without using a rotary compressor.

Scramjet
A supersonic combustion ramjet - scramjet - engine is a ramjet in which air is not decelerated to subsonic speed before combustion.

Shock absorber
A mechanical device designed to smooth out or dampen jarring motions, for example to a car travelling down a bumpy road.

Spark plug
A device that produces an electric spark which ignites the fuel needed in an internal combustion engine.

Spectrometer
An instrument used to determine the chemical composition of a substance by detecting its effect on light passing through or reflected from it.

Surveillance
Secret observation, usually of someone who does not know you are watching them, and would not want you to do so - for example, an enemy in wartime.

Suspension
A system of springs and shock absorbers that connects a vehicle to its wheels. Good suspension provides a comfortable ride and makes the vehicle easier for the driver to handle.

Torque
A way of describing how hard something is turned. Force might be a push or a pull, while torque is a twist.

Turbocharger
A device that sucks extra air into an engine so that it can use fuel more quickly and generate more power

Turbojet
A jet engine containing a device which compresses air. Compression of the air used in internal combustion makes the explosion more powerful.